PRESCHOOL PATHWAYS

PATHWAYS
TO SCIENCE

PRESCHOOL PATHWAYS ᴛᴏ SCIENCE

PrePS™

FACILITATING SCIENTIFIC
WAYS OF THINKING,
TALKING, DOING,
AND UNDERSTANDING

by

Rochel Gelman, Ph.D.
Kimberly Brenneman, Ph.D.
Rutgers University
Piscataway, New Jersey

Gay Macdonald, Ph.D.
UCLA Early Care and Education, Krieger Center
Los Angeles

Moisés Román, M.A.
UCLA Early Care and Education, University Village Center
Los Angeles

·P A U L·H·
BROOKES
PUBLISHING Cᴑ.®

Baltimore • London • Sydney

Paul H. Brookes Publishing Co.
Post Office Box 10624
Baltimore, Maryland 21285-0624
USA

www.brookespublishing.com

Book design by Mindy Dunn.
Typeset by Integrated Publishing Solutions, Grand Rapids, Michigan.
Manufactured in the United States of America by Versa Press, Inc., East Peoria, Illinois.

The individuals described in this book are composites or real people whose situations
are masked and are based on the authors' experiences. In all instances, names and
identifying details have been changed to protect confidentiality.

The photographs in this book are printed with permission of the individuals pictured
or of their parent(s) or legal guardian(s).

Library of Congress Cataloging-in-Publication Data

Gelman, Rochel.
    Preschool pathways to science : facilitating scientific ways of thinking, talking, doing, and
understanding / by Rochel Gelman, Kimberly Brenneman, Gay Macdonald.
        p.   cm.
    Includes bibliographical references and index.
    ISBN-13: 978-1-59857-044-1 (pbk.)
    ISBN-10: 1-59857-044-7
    1. Science—Study and teaching (Preschool) 2. Education, Preschool—Activity programs.
    I. Brenneman, Kimberly. II. Macdonald, Gay. III. Title.
LB1140.5.S35G45   2010
371.3′5–dc22

                                                                                              2009024084

British Library Cataloguing in Publication data are available from the British Library.

2013   2012   2011   2010   2009
10   9   8   7   6   5   4   3   2   1

Contents

List of Figures, Tables, Boxes, and Activities

About the Authors

Rochel Gelman, Ph.D., Professor and Co-Director, Rutgers Center for Cognitive Science and Department of Psychology, 152 Frelinghuysen Road, Piscataway, NJ 08854-8020

Rochel Gelman is a professor of Psychology and Cognitive Science, and the co-director of the Rutgers Center for Cognitive Science (RuCCS). Before joining Rutgers, she was Professor of Psychology first at the University of Pennsylvania and then at the University of California–Los Angeles (UCLA). She is widely known for her pioneering research on what infants and preschool children already know or learn with relative ease. She is a member of the National Academy of Sciences and the American Academy of Arts and Sciences; a William James Fellow of the Association for Psychological Science; and a recipient of the Society for Research in Child Development's Distinguished Lifetime Scientific Contribution to Child Development Award, the Early Career Research Contribution Award, and the Distinguished Scientific Contribution Award of the American Psychological Association. She has received a Mentor Award from Division 7 of the American Psychological Association for her training of other scientists, especially women who have gone on to distinguished careers in psychological research.

Dr. Gelman's research program is organized around a longtime interest in learning, cognition, and developmental cognitive science. Her book, *The Child's Understanding of Number* (Harvard University Press, 1978), with C.R. Gallistel, is considered a landmark publication about preschool children's numerical competencies. Dr. Gelman's other publications include several edited volumes and monographs and more than 100 book chapters and papers. She has collaborated with school and museum professionals in published research on the creation of environments that promote math and science learning in schools and museums. *Preschool Pathways to Science (PrePS™)* represents her most extensive effort of this kind.

Kimberly Brenneman, Ph.D., Assistant Research Professor of Psychology; Professor of Cognitive Development, Rutgers Center for Cognitive Science and Department of Psychology, 152 Frelinghuysen Road, Piscataway, NJ 08854-8020

Kimberly Brenneman is an assistant research professor in the Department of Psychology at Rutgers University. She is also affiliated with the National Institute for Early Education Research (NIEER). In addition to her work on the development, implementation, and assessment of PrePS, Dr. Brenneman's basic research interests include young children's scientific reasoning, their understanding of the relationship between form and function, their comprehension and production of notations, and their understanding of the animate–inanimate distinction. Her work at NIEER focuses on ways to improve the instructional practices that support science and mathematics learning in preschool classrooms. Dr. Brenneman is a regular presenter at national professional conferences, has published a number of research articles, and has served as a board member for multiple community education organizations. She is also an educational consultant to *Sid the Science Kid*, the PBS Kids animated series and web site (produced by KCET/The Jim Henson Company). *Preschool Pathways to Science* is her first book.

Gay Macdonald, Ph.D., Executive Director, UCLA Early Care and Education, Krieger Center, Box 951785, Los Angeles, CA 90095-1785

Gay Macdonald has served as the executive director of UCLA Early Care and Education (ECE) since 1991. She came to this position as a highly experienced and respected child care professional in the Los Angeles community and currently serves on the County of Los Angeles Child Care Planning Committee; she was previously co-chair of the Curriculum Task Team for Los Angeles Universal Preschool. While responsible for the operation of three child care centers at UCLA accredited by the National Association for the Education of Young Children and licensed to serve 340 children ages 2 months to 6 years, Dr. Macdonald always sought ways to expand UCLA's influence in the area of early childhood education throughout the Los Angeles community. Together with the Gelman Cognitive Development Lab, she developed the *Preschool Pathways to Science* program as the integrative focus for all aspects of the ECE program, an innovative approach to providing the highest quality child care for UCLA faculty, staff, and students and a model for the broader community.

Moisés Román, M.A., Director, UCLA Early Care and Education, University Village Center, Box 951785, Los Angeles, CA 90095-1785

Moisés Román is the director of the UCLA Early Care and Education University Village Center. Prior to that assignment, he served as the curriculum coordinator for the department, overseeing the implementation of the science-based curriculum, *Preschool Pathways to Science,* in 19 classrooms and conducting teacher training for all three ECE centers at UCLA. He is an advocate for early childhood education, both for children and for teachers and professionals in the field, and conducts workshops at national, state, and local conferences, presenting a variety of topics such as Science for Young Children, Teachers Matter, Men in Education, the Development of Early Literacy, and many more. Mr. Román also serves as educational consultant to KCET television's award-winning series, *A Place of Our Own/Los Niños en Su Casa,* and to KCET/Jim Henson Company's award-winning PBS Kids series, *Sid the Science Kid.*

Acknowledgments

Preschool Pathways to Science (PrePS™) has been a long time coming—nearly twenty years. It started when NASA approached Gay Macdonald (Executive Director of the sites of the UCLA Early Care and Education [ECE]) with a request to help develop science-learning opportunities for a preschool program serving families at an Air Force base located north of Los Angeles. Gay turned to me, as a member of her advisory board and a student of young children's scientific inclinations. The preparation of the proposal for needed funds was greatly facilitated by the advice I received from my former colleagues at the University of Pennsylvania: Drs. Christine Massey and Pamela Freyd, who had embarked on a related project for kindergarten to Grade 3. Funds in hand, we started. We never anticipated as long a gestation period as proved to be necessary. As a result, we have benefited from the involvement of a very large number of people and schools, teachers, teacher aides, undergraduate and graduate research assistants, and, most especially, the children and their parents or guardians. We are grateful to each and every one of them. Some individuals or groups were critical players in the creation of PrePS. I am deeply grateful for the privilege to work with all of the following individuals:

- Lisa Travis and Earl Williams (members of my lab at UCLA), and Susan Woods (a UCLA teacher), served as project coordinators during the initial years of grant funding from National Aeronautics and Space Administration (NASA; Grant NCC-2826) and the National Science Foundation (NSF; Grant REC-0529579). All understood that the program involved a mind-set shift for the teachers. It was especially important that Susan Wood "got it" from the start and helped other teachers come online. She also worked with Osnat Zur to bring out her children's numerical competence as well as to brainstorm about PrePS. Eventually, Zur filled the same role in meetings with groups of teachers.

- Amy Aguayo, Shabazza Higaro, Jennifer Murillo, Moisés Román, Juanita Salter, Sofia Silva, Fariden Shabanarfar, and Geraldo Soto (all of UCLA ECE) and, again, Lisa Travis, Earl Williams, as well as Osnat Zur, Beth Lavin, Stephanie Reich, and Girlie Delacroix (all at UCLA), showed us some of the many ways that teachers and researchers could work with PrePS at its site of origin. The form of the collaboration that emerged facilitated a related researcher–teacher role as well as the curriculum.

- Ines Louro and Marta Paris (who served as teacher-researchers); Johanna Jandrisovits and Jennifer Manuola (Directors of the Douglass Child Study Center at

Rutgers); Marilyn Valentine (Director, Livingston Avenue Child Development Center); Connie Penn (Director, The Children's Corner)—all based in the New Brunswick, New Jersey area; and Samantha Bundy, Jennifer Cooper, Lindsay Downs, Beth Lavin (who moved to Rutgers), Jaimie Liberty, Kristina Metz, and Irene Nayfeld—members of my lab, all served as key players in the effort to embed PrePS in new schools, including ones serving inner-city families, most of whom were Spanish-speaking.

This creative effort, as well as the preparation of the book, was funded mainly by NSF Grant SBR-9720410. The authors are solely responsible for the opinions and content contained in this book. In no way does our grant support carry an endorsement from the funding agencies.

I now turn to my co-authors. It is hard to imagine anyone who could substitute for Gay Macdonald, Executive Director of the several UCLA ECE sites. She understood immediately that we were taking on a hard task. Still, she put her full trust in me, probably knowing that this would draw me in as it did. This is but one sign of why Gay is a brilliant leader and mentor. Early on in our work, she identified the then very young Moisés Román as a winner. He became a key member of the conceptual team in very short order. Both Gay and Moisés have served as editors, reviewers, and rewriters throughout the preparation of this book. At every step of the way, Kimberly Brenneman has been a fantastic colleague and friend as well as an unbelievably fine collaborator. We became close to one mind as the book took final shape. This was very much facilitated by Kim's role as project organizer—and thus overseer—of the successful effort to move PrePS from its development to its implementation into on-going programs, including programs for children from different economic strata. As a result, we learned a great deal about how to help teachers get started with and then continue to use PrePS. What a wonderful team of authors! Thank you. Thank you.

Rochel Gelman
July 2009

In memory of
Ann L. Brown

Introduction to PrePS™

Young children can demonstrate surprisingly abstract abilities, as did Dara (3 years 11 months) who denied that a puppet could remember but allowed that a cat could. When asked why, she answered, "because all the things that are alive can remember." In a related way, when 3- and 4-year-olds were shown photographs of a statue that had human-like features, they said that it could not go up and down a hill by itself. In contrast, they accurately judged that an echidna, an animal they had never seen or heard about, could move by itself. When asked to explain, children said that the statue was "just a furniture-animal," that it did not have "real" feet, or that it was "too shiny." However, they said the echidna, which looked more like a cactus than any familiar animal, could move by itself "because it had feet"—even though these were under the echidna and not visible.

These vignettes are consistent with the growing research base that shows that young children, including infants, can treat the difference between animate and inanimate objects in an abstract way (e.g., Gelman & Opfer, 2002; Saxe, Tzelnic, & Carey, 2007) and shows children reaching inferences on the basis of high-level knowledge. Indeed, the book *Eager to Learn* (Bowman, Donovan, & Burns, 2001) summarizes the evidence as follows:

> [There] appear to be "privileged domains" [of learning], that is, domains in which children have a natural proclivity to learn, experiment and explore . . . [T]hey allow for nurturing and extending the boundaries of the learning in which children are already actively engaged. (p. 9)

Reports from the National Academy of Science (Duschl, Schweingruber, & Shouse, 2006) the National Science Board (2009), and various private foundations concur: Science learning opportunities should be strengthened in early education. The Bowman et al. (2001) report details efforts to uncover what preschool children can do in the realm of abstract thinking as opposed to what they cannot do. The "can-do" research base is the bedrock of our program—Preschool Pathways to Science (PrePS™)—and informs our design of appropriate science-learning opportunities for preschool children.

These research and policy developments present a challenge to educators committed to assumptions of traditional stage theories, which characterize young children as being perception-bound and unable to engage in abstract thinking. Many educators, therefore, may believe that young children do not benefit from classroom

1

opportunities that ask them to engage in abstract thinking and are best served when given materials for their own hands-on exploratory play (Elkind, 1989).

It is true that preschoolers—as well as elementary and high school students, and even some adults—are not ready to assimilate certain aspects of science and math. For example, lessons about the Newtonian principles of physics and the biochemistry of diseases do not guarantee learning on the part of college students (e.g., McCloskey, Washburn, & Felch, 1983). However, preschoolers can understand or learn about some areas of science with relative ease. As discussed in the Bowman et al. (2001) report, science-learning opportunities fit well with children's active tendencies to explore, seek information, and try out different ways to use materials. Furthermore, learning how to do science also provides literacy and arithmetic experiences.

SCIENCE FOR PRESCHOOL?

Some people may think that we are being overly optimistic about the abilities of preschool children. After all, traditional stage theory continues to be taught to future educators. Piaget (1970), Vygotsky (1962), and Bruner (1964) all share the view that young children are perception-bound and lack the mental structures needed to interpret abstract relations. Because of a dependence on the "here and now," children do not use consistent criteria on classification tasks, fail conservation of number and volume tasks, engage in precausal reasoning, and often rely on their own egocentric perspective to judge the perspectives of others. Even when children in the early elementary grades progress to Piaget's stage of concrete operations and begin to sort objects according to a consistent set of logical criteria and to systematically rank-order objects with different lengths, they still are characterized as lacking the basic cognitive capacity to understand the methods and content of science (Inhelder & Piaget, 1964). Vygotsky (1962) concluded that children could not engage in scientific reasoning until they are about 10–12 years old.

There are reliable research findings to support the stage theorists' assumptions for the preschool years. Piaget's liquid conservation experiment provides a compelling example. Four-year-olds almost always fail the Piagetian conservation test. Even though they watch as the water in one of two identical glasses of water is poured into a taller and thinner glass, they assert that the resulting amounts are no longer equal. They justify their nonconserving answer by saying that there is more in the tall column of water. When the water in the tall column is returned to its original glass, children assert that there now is the same amount of water as there was to start. Older children conserve the original amount as it is transferred to the glass with different dimensions. This is an especially salient example of how preschool children can be captured by the perceptual here and now. There are many others (Gelman & Baillargeon, 1983).

Given that there are ample demonstrations of young children being misled by the surface characteristics of objects, people might reasonably ask, "Why develop a preschool program about science?" Our answer is that young children are "scientists-in-waiting." They are naturally curious and actively involved in exploring the world around them. More to the point, they can and do develop abstract concepts in domains that fall within the content of science. As illustrated above, young children are well along in their learning about the animate-inanimate distinction. In

PrePS we link conceptual accomplishments like these to the development of process skills that are important for science, including *observing, comparing and contrasting, measuring, predicting, checking, recording,* and *reporting.* Classroom teachers serve a key role in modeling, guiding, and supporting these skills for young children. We will further explore the value of PrePS for children and their teachers in the remainder of this chapter and throughout the book.

MORE COMPETENCE THAN MEETS THE EYE

We are fortunate to work in a time when the preschool mind is celebrated for what it can do rather than what it cannot do. Preschoolers were once thought to be conceptually limited, but research has since demonstrated that they are able to think and talk about many science-related topics (Carey, 2009; Gopnik & Schulz, 2007).

When children are provided with opportunities to further develop a knowledge base they know something about already, they can perform in rather sophisticated ways. For example, Novak and Gowin (1984) reported that some second-grade students who participated in an elementary science tutorial program achieved a better grasp of the particulate nature of matter than did some 12th-grade students. These researchers concluded that schools were failing to take advantage of young children's science-learning capacity. We agree and submit that the same is true for even younger children.

You may already know that some preschoolers are dinosaur experts and can name an impressive number of dinosaurs. When certain children encounter a picture of a novel dinosaur, they may even be able to tell you what it ate and where it lived. As Gobbo and Chi (1986) demonstrated, these budding young experts organize their knowledge in this domain in a hierarchical fashion. When children observe that a dinosaur has large, sharp teeth, they then infer that the animal is a carnivore—and even use the technical term *carnivore.* A related demonstration comes from some children's motivation to learn about Pokémon characters, so much so that they know more than their parents about the interrelationships and features of the characters (Lavin, Galotti, & Gelman, 2003).

A new generation of cognitive developmental researchers has embraced the idea that preschoolers' concepts are often more advanced than previously believed (see Chapter 2). This has led to a major focus on identifying preschoolers' conceptual competence. There is an ever-growing body of evidence that preschool children actively build a knowledge system around the principled distinction between animate and inanimate objects and related concepts of causality. For example, when asked what is inside a doll, an animal, and a person, a very large majority of 3-year-old children provide fundamentally different answers for each kind of object: The doll has stuff, batteries, or even air inside, whereas animals and people (Gelman, 1990; Gottfried & Gelman, 2004) have blood, bones, food, and even *character* (what a 5-year-old child volunteered to Brenneman) on their insides. Results like these contributed to our decision to develop PrePS. The difference between animate and inanimate objects and their differential conditions for motion and change are foundational for science. In addition, the animate-inanimate findings provide powerful evidence that young children can make inductions from what is known to what is not known, to think about the unseen, and to organize knowledge into hierarchical structures.

Other similar sets of findings about preschool conceptual competence contributed to the decision to develop PrePS.

We know now, for example, that preschool-age children can reason about cause and effect. An early study by Bullock and Gelman (1979) showed that children make reasonable choices about potential causes and assume that causes precede effects. This is but one result that contradicts Piaget's (1930) view that young children are precausal because they lack an assumption of mechanism, confuse the order of cause and effect, and attribute animate powers to all objects. For example, Laura Schulz and Elizabeth Bonawitz (2007) found that preschoolers are motivated to seek explanations through exploration. Under normal circumstances, preschoolers will stop playing with an old toy when a novel one is offered. In the Schulz and Bonawitz work, preschoolers did just this when the mechanism that made the toy work was clear to them. When this mechanism was not understood, however, children tended to ignore the second toy and continue to explore the first toy until they figured out how the toy worked. The simple presence of a new toy did not outweigh their motivation to reach closure on their goal to understand. This example illustrates an important characteristic of young children. They are motivated to continue to repeat an activity or to ask questions until they get the information they are seeking (Chouinard, 2007). Somehow they monitor their own knowledge and continue to explore, providing repeated evidence that the young mind is, indeed, active and engaged.

Given the ever-growing research base about preschoolers' competence, we set out to determine how to leverage children's spontaneous explorations and knowledge-seeking activities about some science concepts to create a program to support preschool science learning. Why resist the opportunity to move children onto relevant learning paths for science? Some preschool educators may offer an answer to this question: They were not required to study science and do not feel prepared to teach it. Nor are they eager to add yet another set of activities to their already full agendas.

Many teachers are concerned about their ability to teach science. However, because the science used in PrePS is based on what has been learned about preschool minds, the selected topics are not examples of a pushdown curriculum from physics, chemistry, or microbiology. Teachers will also find that they can embed some aspects of PrePS into what they are doing without much additional effort. They will be able to use science to encourage children to ask questions, solve problems, communicate and pay attention to detail, record observations and predictions, learn the terms that describe their observations, and use these terms across lessons. For us, the best evidence that preschool teachers can work with and benefit from PrePS is that many come to realize that they do know a lot about the science and, like their children, are eager to learn more.

A PREVIEW OF PrePS

PrePS encourages science-based learning through activities and experiences that allow children to explore big ideas in depth and to learn the practices and language of science. The program was designed to enhance the classroom experience for both teachers and children. Preschool teachers, directors, and cognitive researchers collaborated with the goal of fostering enthusiasm, fresh perspectives, and feelings of competence in the classroom. From the teacher's point of view, PrePS can ease the typical workload by encouraging collaboration and connecting daily lesson plans.

We are determined to feed the curiosity of young children and capitalize on their tendencies to actively explore their social and physical worlds. Therefore, PrePS makes a special effort to develop children's observational skills for purposes of obtaining information in a reliable way—through their own observations and explorations of the world but also through discussions with classmates and teachers and by engaging in simple experiments. The program also features teachers' support of children's tendencies to ask questions and make predictions about topics related to science. We want children to learn that a question might have more than one answer. Most important, PrePS is a program that places the development of scientific processes in the context of the need to develop connections between concepts and the related vocabulary across learning experiences throughout the year. Children are encouraged to draw connections between activities, ideas, and vocabulary; to link questions and solutions from one activity to another; and to understand and relate transformations and sequences that unfold over time, as in the case of plant and animal life cycles.

PrePS teachers connect learning experiences throughout the school year based on a key principle of learning: It is always easier to learn something that one already knows something about than to start from scratch (Bransford, Brown, & Cocking, 1999; Gelman & Lucariello, 2002; Resnick, 1987). This principle applies to all learners, especially young ones. For example, a 4-year-old boy went to a science program for young children at the Franklin Institute in Philadelphia. When asked what he learned at program, the child replied, "I learned when they evacuated a tube, things fell together." No amount of questioning elicited another answer. But later in middle school, the boy related what he learned in school that day by tying it to his memory from preschool: "Remember when I went to the Franklin Institute and we evacuated that tube? Well, now I know what that was all about." It is our hope that your students will learn enough to make comparable connections at a later point in their education. The goal is to put the children on relevant learning paths that will provide more and more relevant data for constructing coherent understandings.

PrePS allows teachers to systematically plan their curricula and set specific, attainable learning goals for their students. Teachers can guide children in organized investigations of the everyday world, thus promoting scientific skills such as observing, predicting, checking, measuring, comparing, recording, and explaining. Although subsequent chapters in this book provide examples of how we have introduced these activities, it is important to realize that PrePS is not a set curriculum with fixed units that must be taught in sequence, or a list of unrelated facts and terms that children must master. Rather, PrePS is an approach that relies on the natural curiosity and flexibility of preschool children and teachers.

When implementing PrePS, you will not be asked to prepare seat-work. You will not encounter a pushdown curriculum that is made up of bits and pieces of what is found in textbooks for much older students, nor will you be put in the position of simply teaching children to memorize facts and words. Programs that offer pushdown ideas for science activities often require that learners already have sophisticated levels of background knowledge. Although young children can observe such things as the shape of the moon, they cannot be expected to understand why the moon changes shape, its 28-day cycle, its effect on the tides, or why people would weigh less if they were on the moon.

With PrePS, you will be embedding appropriate key content and science practices across the curriculum. You will be able to take advantage of the fact that concepts do not stand alone, each separate from the other. In this way, you can build sequences of learning experiences that help children construct conceptually coherent domains of knowledge about particular science topics. For example, consider the concept of *animal*. Such a thing moves by itself, breathes, eats, reproduces, and grows. Many of the same terms can be applied to trees and other plants; however, plants cannot move around by themselves and do not obtain nourishment in the same way as animals. Even some 3-year-olds recognize this distinction (Gelman, 2003; Inagaki & Hatano, 2002).

Preschool children are able to deal with abstract concepts, as we discuss further in Chapter 2. The examples presented throughout the book illustrate the deep interrelationship between concepts and their related verbal descriptions. Consider the word *bat*, which refers to two very different concepts: *a nocturnal animal* and *a sports tool*. The different interpretations lead to very different inferences. For example, if someone tells you, "The bat is made of wood," you could infer that it is long, rigid, and used to hit balls. You would not infer that it eats, has babies, flies at night, and has good hearing.

PrePS incorporates lessons learned from extensive research on the acquisition of organized knowledge, which is fostered when learners are offered 1) multiple examples of the content and tools of a domain and 2) repeated opportunities to use the practices of the domain (Brown & Campione, 1996; Dunbar & Fugelsang, 2005; Gelman, 1998). PrePS also takes advantage of preschoolers' propensity to repeat a given task until they are satisfied with their own level of performance. Box 1.1 provides a particularly compelling example of this internal motivation.

Box 1.1
SPONTANEOUS SELF-CORRECTION

Annette Karmiloff-Smith and Barbel Inhelder (1974) designed a study in which preschool- and elementary-age children were given multiple opportunities to balance various blocks on top of a metal rod. Children assumed that all the blocks balanced at their geometric center but soon discovered that some blocks violated this rule. As the session progressed, the children adjusted their balancing strategies, moving from guesswork and random trial-and-error methods to purposeful attempts to determine which side of the block provided the best balance point. PrePS draws from a key finding: Children kept trying different solutions, even when this meant giving up a working strategy for one that did not work as well at first. Children went beyond simply making blocks balance to trying to figure out a rule for balancing. It is noteworthy that children were able to use the same blocks over and over again. However, if the authors had not weighted blocks in odd ways, it is unlikely that the children would have been motivated to search for a particular kind of rule (e.g., how to balance the blocks that looked alike but had different insides).

Many children have a habit of counting something over and over again, including steps, cracks in the sidewalk, or the number of telephone poles they pass while riding in the car. Children also are self-motivated to repeat a given activity. The extent to which these tendencies are engaged is critically related to the kinds of environments children encounter. If children are not offered a variety of environments that are about science, they are not likely to invent them. Even if they do invent such environments, there is no guarantee that children will know how to use and think about them. PrePS teachers serve a critical guiding role by providing children with repeated (ubiquitous), related (redundant) opportunities to work with a concept and to explore it scientifically. Redundancy and ubiquity foster organized learning.

Figure 1.1 provides an example of the principles of redundancy and ubiquity at work in the PrePS program. In September, a class of 4-year-old children traced one of their shoes. When the children were asked how large the shoe was, they had some difficulty answering. This same activity was repeated whenever each child got larger shoes so that throughout the year, children made multiple shoe entries in their science journals. They also learned to write numerals and to use a date stamp appropriately. These developments were due to the ubiquitous embedding of measuring and dating activities in various science-learning opportunities and clearly contributed to a shift in the quality of entries in the children's science journals. As seen in Figure 1.1A, at the start of the school year, one child decorated her shoe with hearts and stamped the date all over the page. When asked how large her shoe was, the child told her teacher that she did not know. Later in the year, before the child measured her new shoe, her teacher asked her to make a prediction. By this point in the school year, she was able to do so. Furthermore, after she measured her shoe, she spontaneously wrote the numerals along its right side (see Figure 1.1B). The child's spontaneous use of numbers is also noteworthy because she related them to measuring. By looking across journal entries, one can document progress in literacy and drawing skills. Journals become a noninvasive source of information about a child's progress during the school year.

Figure 1.1 illustrates another key feature of the PrePS program: ensuring that there are science tools in the everyday environment. Although preschoolers are self-motivated to question and discover, they often are unfamiliar with the physical tools (e.g., rulers, magnifying glasses, weights and scales, date stamps) and specific vocabulary of science (e.g., *observe, predict, research, record*). PrePS provides experiences that allow children to use these tools and words in simple but correct ways. As the year progresses, children start to understand how to use these tools and words independently because of multiple opportunities to use them with help from adults.

Although PrePS emphasizes the development of scientific thought, it encompasses many other social and cognitive skills: math and number abilities, early literacy and language skills, social communication, and emotional sensitivity. Mathematical skills are supported as children count, measure, and compare quantities while doing science. Likewise, literacy is enhanced as children record and date their observations and ask for books that can answer their questions. Science also requires children to think critically and to compare and contrast evidence from different sources.

Investigative activities help to develop abilities that go far beyond the scope of what one traditionally considers as science. PrePS strengthens basic decision-making and problem-solving skills, thus allowing children to seek and interpret information for themselves rather than to simply accept what authorities offer. Science requires

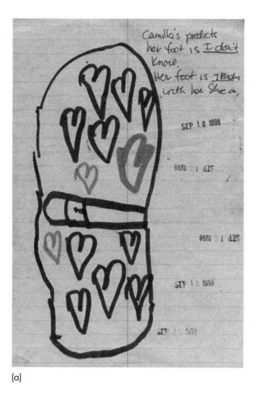
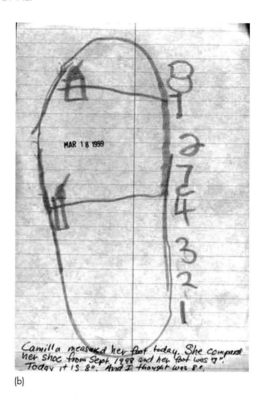

(a)   (b)

Figure 1.1. Journal entry, before and after PrePS experience.

teamwork among individuals who encourage and respect the opinions of others. Sharing, respect for others and their ideas, and cooperation are necessary social skills for both scientists and preschoolers. This broader conception of science provides a lens through which to view and reevaluate typical preschool activities. Many opportunities for science activities already exist in preschool classrooms. For example, storytime can include nonfiction science books or stories with a science theme (see Chapter 3 for suggestions). If teachers include sharing time in the classroom schedule, they can guide children's sharing choices so that they relate to a topic under study. For example, as part of an investigation of the science concept of *change*, children can bring in "something that changes." Children's choices—which in our experiences have included a wide range of objects including a transforming toy, a flashlight, a change of clothes, and ice cubes—create an opportunity to discuss what change means and how much they already know about it. Box 1.2 illustrates how children and teachers can explore scientific ideas together during group time.

When science is understood as a process of studying the objects and events in the world by asking and answering questions, the scientific process can be integrated throughout the school day and included in a wide range of activities. Science is not a collection of unrelated activities that are inserted into particular time slots in a classroom schedule. One central tenet of the PrePS program is that experience and learning in one area leads to learning and understanding in conceptually related areas. For example, when learning about the human body, children may explore the form and function of different body parts (e.g., the shape and purpose of the teeth, joints, stomach, brain, legs, and heart). When children start thinking about the bod-

---

Box 1.2
DO INSECTS HAVE HEARTS?

As part of their exploration of insides and outsides, children were asked to think about what might be inside ants and cockroaches and to predict what was the same about them. One child suggested that both insects have hearts inside, but another child disagreed so the teacher asked the class to vote. Although all of his classmates agreed that ants and cockroaches have hearts, the lone dissenter stood his ground. This sparked a discussion about what kinds of things have hearts. One child reasoned that ants and cockroaches are living things and that all living things have hearts. Another child pointed out that plants are alive but do not have hearts. After hearing his classmates' ideas, the skeptical child suggested doing research to find a definitive answer.

The children in this classroom were learning science facts (e.g., ants and cockroaches are living things) and science vocabulary (e.g., *research*). They used critical thinking skills (e.g., plants are alive, yet they do not have hearts) to produce relevant information. This example also illustrates how PrePS encourages social and emotional development: One child possessed the self-confidence to express an opinion that differed from that of the class, and the other students respected his differing opinion.

---

ies of other kinds of animals, they will learn more effectively because they can build on what they already know and draw connections between one area of investigation (e.g., the shape and purpose of human body parts) and another (e.g., the shape and purpose of animal body parts). As children start to acquire new information and to apply knowledge across different areas, they feel pride in their sense of understanding and joy in making discoveries. They have the satisfaction of being active collaborators in their own education. These moments inspire children to learn more and to work together toward the goal of discovery.

As you read this book, you may be reminded of some or all of the following concepts:

1. Emergent curriculum, with the teacher as facilitator and not lecturer

2. Active, hands-on exploration

3. The integrated day

4. Webbing

5. The Reggio Emilia program (Wurm, 2005)

6. Montessori

7. Vygotsky and the zone of proximal development

8. Piaget's view of children as active learners who construct their understanding of the world

Indeed, we have been influenced by many aspects of other programs and theories, especially when these overlap with our ideas for doing and thinking about science. Many preschool teachers are already including some of the elements of PrePS in their classrooms by encouraging children to ask questions, solve problems, communicate, work and play in groups, and pay attention to details. These are thinking skills that can be applied to a variety of content domains, but their use and content will vary. For example, if children are having a pretend tea party, they need to select objects that are relevant to the script, such as a toy teapot, small cups, and tiny spoons. With science, the props should be items that encourage exploration and thinking about the nature of objects in the world.

In PrePS, science is not a rigid set of sophisticated experiments, formulas, and rules. Rather, *science* refers to an attitude—an intellectual approach to viewing the natural world—with an investigative method of asking and answering questions (and a willingness to entertain alternative explanations). Implementing PrePS requires changes in the conceptual approach to teaching, but it does not necessarily entail a comprehensive overhaul of the learning environment. As the teacher, you will be thinking and investigating (and encouraging the children to think and investigate) in ways that are increasingly structured, cooperative, and conceptually focused.

Chapter 2 reviews more topic areas about which preschool children know and, as Bowman et al. (2001) put it, are "eager to learn." It also describes the PrePS framework that can guide you and your students through conceptually connected learning experiences. Chapter 3 outlines how to use science practices with different content. Chapter 4 discusses the use of PrePS throughout the year, either as a primary or complementary program. Finally, Chapter 5 delves into issues of assessment.

CONCLUSION

Some key ideas permeate this book. First, in learning science, knowledge about the world is related to the practices and tools of science. Together, the conceptual–language side and the practice–tool side form a coherent approach to how science is characterized and carried out.

In teaching the conceptual–language aspect of science, the following items should be considered:

1. Concepts do not stand alone; they are organized in a coherent way and support inferences.

2. Understanding of vocabulary is related to understanding of related concepts. In a sense, concepts and their related terms are opposite sides of the same coin.

3. If one already has some knowledge about a concept, further learning about that concept is facilitated.

4. Young children use what they know to participate actively in their own learning.

5. Young children have organized knowledge about some core domains (see Chapter 2).

6. Providing multiple and related examples to young children gives them the opportunity to engage actively in concept and language learning. Withholding such opportunities is akin to producing a deprivation environment.

7. Redundant and ubiquitous opportunities to work with a concept and its language are critical conditions for conceptual development, but this takes time and planning on the part of the teacher.

8. Planning activities and learning experiences that are connected to one another helps children find these connections.

When teaching science practices, the following items should be considered:

1. Careful observations are needed to gain information.

2. Predicting and checking are fundamental science practices.

3. Comparing and contrasting are also fundamental practices; they can lead to the idea of a variable.

4. Data should be recorded by drawing, writing, and using numerals to represent them.

5. Work should be dated.

6. Scientific vocabulary should be used in context.

7. The environment should be filled with tools (e.g., rulers and measuring devices, magnifiers). Guidance about using tools, along with opportunities to do so, should be provided.

8. Opportunities for children to communicate about their findings should be provided.

9. Take time with new concepts, ideas, and skills. Be patient as you encourage children to practice, explore, and build understanding.

2

The Nature and Development of Concepts

IMPLICATIONS FOR TEACHING PRESCHOOL SCIENCE

Alex: (3 years old) "What dat mean? The car is dead?"
Mom: "Why?"
Alex: "Cars can't die."
Mom: "Why not?"
Alex: "Not people."
Mom: "So?"
Alex: "People make cars go. Cars can't."

In his early work, Piaget (1930) interviewed children of different ages about their understandings about objects and events in the world. One conclusion he drew is that preschool-age children are universal animists because of their tendencies to attribute life to almost anything in the world, including bicycles, mountains, and the sun. In general, developmental theories tell us that preschool children are not able to form abstract concepts, make inferences, distinguish living items from nonliving ones, or understand counterfactuals. The nature of Alex's reasoning, however, is clearly at odds with the attribution of animism and traditional developmental theories (Gelman & Baillargeon, 1983). Recall that preschool children are especially good at distinguishing between and reasoning about key aspects of animate and inanimate objects (see Chapter 1).

Additional findings about the distinction between animate and inanimate objects—for both infants and preschool children—are summarized by Gelman and Opfer (2002). Work by Poulin-Dubois (1999) provided a compelling example of the evidence from experiments with 9- and 12-month-old children. She demonstrated that infants of both ages were surprised when they saw a robot move by itself—something inanimate objects cannot do. A related finding is provided by Spelke, Phillips, and Woodward (1995). These authors had infants watch one of two events: 1) a person moved sideways and stopped before reaching a second person, at which point the second person moved sideways away from the first individual; or 2) a block of the same height, width, and depth moved sideways before reaching a second block of the same size, at which point the latter block moved away from the first block. In both cases, there was no contact between the pair of objects. Infants were surprised to see a block move by itself, whereas they took the first event in stride. This suggests that infants expect that inanimate objects will not interact at a distance to produce a cause–effect sequence. In contrast, they are not surprised when the cause of motion of an animate entity seems to come from within; this is expected (Baillargeon, Yu, Yuan, Li, & Luo, 2009).

Results of this sort conflict with the set of findings that are used to support a traditional, stage-theory approach to development. How do we reconcile them? The answer is related to the developmental theory within which individuals work.

MORE ABOUT THEORIES

In the learning and cognitive sciences, considerable attention is given to the distinction between domain-general and domain-specific theories of knowledge acquisition. Information processing theory is an example of a domain-general commitment, in which emphasis is placed on the conditions that influence processes such as working memory, processing speed, attention, inhibition, recognition, recall, and forgetting (Kail, 2007; Munakata, 2006; Perlmutter, 1980). Development is related to increases in the ability to use these processes. For example, as processing speed increases, so does the amount of information children can take in for a given interval of time. The buildup of knowledge is assumed to be due to the process of association under conditions that favor association strength. From a developmental perspective, the assumption is that knowledge grows as a function of the opportunity to associate the sensory or perceptual data that are made available by inputs from the world and builds bit by bit or component by component. Within this framework, the task for the teacher is to encourage children to acquire perceptions and skills that are critical to the teacher's outcome goals.

Stage theories, often called *developmental theories,* also exemplify domain-general accounts of cognitive development (Bruner, 1964; Inhelder & Piaget, 1964; Vygotsky, 1962). They are committed to the view that everyone, including infants, has a strong tendency to interact with and learn about the world. Further, they agree that available mental structures influence what learners notice and assimilate. Although infants are granted a motivation to learn from the start, they are not granted initial cognitive biases or structures that facilitate learning. The crowning achievement of this stage is the development, around 2 years of age, of a mental structure that allows the child to begin to think symbolically. This enables the learner to re-represent and, therefore, recall the past, imitate, engage in pretend play, treat objects as continuing to exist when they are out of sight, and begin to use words with meaning. The assumption is that these different accomplishments of the sensorimotor stage are due to a new, common kind of mental format or structure. This achievement leads into the perceptual stage, the one that is our particular focus. According to Piaget's description of the mind, preschool children should fail a number of conceptual tasks, and they do (e.g., Piaget, 1952). Preschool children fail both classification and conservation tasks. When given a set of blocks that vary in shape and color, a logical organization of them would involve placing all the red and only the red blocks in one pile, all the blue and only the blue blocks in another pile, and so on. Instead, children make objects, like a train or a house or start out by placing two yellow blocks together and then switching to match the shape of one of the blocks, and so on (Inhelder & Piaget, 1964). Bruner (1964) and Vygotsky (1962) used somewhat different tasks but reported the same kind of data.

The well-known Piagetian number conservation task, along with the liquid amount conservation task reviewed in Chapter 1, adds to the examples of preschool children relying on perceptual data to solve a reasoning problem. For example, when a 4-year-old girl watched an adult place two rows of chips so that the items were across from each other, she agreed that both rows had the same number of chips. Then, as she watched, the adult spread out one row and asked again if both rows had the same number. Now, the child said that the longer row had more chips than the other. Apparently, the change in length for one row was sufficient for her to deny the continued numerical equivalence across the two sets of objects. Perhaps even more surprising, when the longer row was changed back to its original configuration, the child said that, once again, both rows had the same number. Changing the items to pennies, cookies, flowers, or toys has no effect. In all cases, it is as if the act of spreading suffices to change the number of items in a collection. In about 2 or 3 years, when the same child watched a video of her younger self, she was flabbergasted. Like other 6- or 7-year-old children, she now conserved number across the irrelevant transformation of length. Often, children of this age will look at the adult asking the questions as if to say, "Why are you bothering me with so obvious a fact?" Indeed, the first author well remembers when a 6-year-old child looked up at her and said, "Lady, is this really how you make a living?" (See Gelman & Baillargeon, 1983, for a review of other studies by stage theorists.)

Preschool programs based on traditional stage theory encourage hands-on activities with props, ones that are meant to provide the kind of exploration that eventually supports the use of mental structures of classification, ordering (sticks, steps, circles of different lengths or widths), the conservation of quantities, and other abstract concepts. In these programs, there are opportunities to pour liquids and sand, play with blocks that can be classified, and so forth. If teachers work within the framework of Bruner or Vygotsky, they also will focus on the development of language and conversational skills. A teacher's ability to do this takes advantage of an already considerable ability of young children—their competence with language and conversation.

When children start to talk, they learn about 9 words per day (Carey, 1985; Miller, 1977; Templin, 1957) and have a vocabulary of around 10,000 words by the first grade. They also show considerable conversational skills. The conversation initiated by Alex at the start of this chapter is a good example of the conversational competence of preschool children when the topic is something they know or want to learn about (Danby, 2002; Shatz & Gelman, 1973; Siegal & Surian, 2004).

An example of this conversational skill was reported in a study by Gelman and Shatz (1977). When 4-year-old children took on the task of explaining a complicated toy to a 2-year-old child, a peer, and an adult, they adjusted the length of their utterances, vocabulary, and syntax depending on the age (and assumed level of understanding) of their partner. For example, when the 4-year-old children talked to 2-year-old children, they used short sentences with a large number of attentional items (e.g., "lookit") and commands (e.g., "put it here"). When the same children talked to an adult, they used longer sentences than they did with their peers. They also used sociolinguistic ways to mark the recognition of status: One child said, "I think that you can put the gas in here" to an adult, but "You can put the gas in here" to a peer. The use of "I think that" was a way to acknowledge that the listener knows much more. Early learning of ways to mark relative status is common across languages. When introduced to an Italian-speaking 4-year-old child, the first author used the formal version of a common greeting. The child turned around and, with more than a little bit of disdain, responded by offering (in a teaching voice) the informal version of a greeting. The child knew that the latter was the correct sociolinguistic rule for an adult to talk to a child.

Preschool children who engage in relatively complex conversations are demonstrating another example of early competence. This competence falls within the over-arching domain of sociality, which guides children's learning about their roles as social beings. To demonstrate conversational competence, one must know something about the topic at hand, take another's perspective into account, and respond to the conversational partner in a relevant way. It is easy to produce egocentric talk in adults—just ask them to tell another person about a topic about which he or she is ignorant. The same applies for children. As long as children can talk about things that they understand, they are able to adjust their messages for different people and contexts. Recall Alex's question, "What dat mean, the car is dead?" It should be clear now that the question was motivated by the child's knowledge about an abstract difference between animate and inanimate objects, and therefore the appropriateness of particular statements. In his understanding, "dead" was not a word or concept that applied to things like cars. This brings us to the need to consider the kind of developmental theory that can accommodate such findings of early competence.

The domain-specific theory of cognitive development is based on the idea that there are some content domains or areas that young children, and even babies, actively engage and learn about (see Chapter 1). The domain-specific account (Gelman & Lucariello, 2002; Gelman & Williams, 1998; Spelke & Kinzler, 2007) shares with developmental theorists (e.g., Bruner, 1964; Gibson, 1970; Piaget, 1970) the assumption that young children are born to learn. However, it breaks with domain-general stage theories by granting young learners skeletal knowledge structures for some particular content areas, including social interaction, number and quantity, space, some topics in biology, and knowledge about physical objects.

We use the metaphor of skeletal knowledge structures to illustrate the idea that core domains are learned with relative ease. It suggests that existing knowledge is at best an outline of what it will be, but it provides a foundational structure for further development. As we have discussed, everyone has a tendency to learn more about what they already know, so it is efficient for learning that the mind comes ready to learn. It uses existing structures, no matter how skeletal they might be, to find and assimilate data in the environment that can put flesh on each potential body of knowledge. The effect is the buildup of particular structure-relevant knowledge (e.g., Gelman & Williams, 1998; Spelke, 2000).[1]

Among these core domains is natural number (the counting numbers), which is organized in terms of discrete number concepts and the operations of addition, sub-

[1] Core domains are distinguished from non-core domains that are learned much later in school and often with great difficulty (Gelman, 2009). Still, in each case different domains feature different core concepts and organizing principles.

traction, and ordering (Dehaene & Changeux, 1993; Gallistel & Gelman, 2005). Because the concept of cardinal number is independent of item type or features, a child can count a collection regardless of its composition, be the items chairs, children who came to school that day, friends, or spaces left at the lunch table. Teachers, therefore, should encourage children to count heterogeneous sets, compare their counts, and think about the effects of adding and subtracting. Many preschool number programs are lacking recommendations to relate counts to arithmetic and ordering, although the literature provides no reason to restrict number experience to counting (Campbell, 2006; Gelman & Gallistel, 1978).

In the domain of causality, things are organized differently. The concern here is the nature of things in the world and how they change and move. If one wants to move an object, it is necessary to know how large and heavy it is, whether it can go down a flight of stairs, and whether it is moving toward you. The core domain of space is concerned about places in a given layout and the geometry that organizes the distance and angles between them and the surrounding boundary. These can even win out over attributes that characterize moveable landmarks (Cheng & Newcombe, 2005; Hermer & Spelke, 1996). The best evidence that geometric variables serve this domain comes from studies where children or adults are first shown a distinctive object in a given place in a rectangular room with one brightly colored wall, then blindfolded and turned around several times, and finally asked to point to or walk to the object. Under these conditions, everyone uses the geometric information of the room but not the landmark colored wall. So, for example, if the object was near the place where a long wall on the right and short wall on the back of the room intersect, then individuals point in either this direction or the one that is kitty-corner; that is, the geometrically equivalent one. We all have experiences that help highlight this important result whenever we emerge from a building and start walking in the wrong direction. After a while, you notice that the landmarks are wrong. Now you have to turn around 180 degrees. The first move relied on your implicit geometric knowledge, and it took a while for you to pay attention to landmarks. The assumption that young children do the same has an implication for teaching. This is that children can be encouraged to try to draw maps to represent the walks they take. These can even be trips from one room to another. When we have done this with children, we have been pleased by how much they enjoy the activity. The first author had her undergraduate class track changes in 4-year-old children's maps as a function of repeated opportunities to take a walk around the outside of their class. With some hints to pay attention to what is attached to the ground or is not moveable, there was a noticeable improvement in the children's maps.

A key feature of the domain-specific approach is that it recognizes that different domains can call for different ways of treating the same objects. For example, the material from which an object is made does not matter when one is counting. The principles of the domain of number apply regardless of material kind. On the other hand, substance matters quite a bit when one makes judgments about the animacy status of a novel object in the world. Concepts do not stand alone; they are organized in ways that support predictions and inferences.

Because the domains that children know something about converge upon domains that are a resource for preschool science, it is not surprising that there is a growing crescendo to provide science-learning experiences for young children (e.g., Gardner, 1991). Preschool Pathways to Science (PrePS™) grows from the theoretical commitment to the active learner who already has some foundational competence with core domains. We therefore decided to apply the domain-specific approach to early science instruction to help teachers help children learn in ways that extend their existing knowledge.

THEORY INTO PRACTICE

In adapting the lessons of the domain-specific approach to the development of PrePS, we want to provide educational opportunities that build on the knowledge children already have to support them as they build further coherent knowledge about science concepts. Recall that two key ideas about domain-specific theories are 1) concepts, language, and their use are interrelated; and 2) it is easier for young children to learn more about what they already know than to learn unconnected material. For these reasons, teachers should offer multiple, organized learning experiences that are conceptually connected by a "big science idea." Allowing children to practice thinking, talking, and working with a concept over time builds deeper understanding.

DEVELOPING THE PrePS FRAMEWORK

> It is not about what, as a teacher, do I want the children to be doing, but what do I want the children to be *thinking* about . . . .Then (I ask myself), what should they be doing to better understand the concept?
>
> —JS, PrePS teacher

We call a big science idea a *central concept* (i.e., what the teacher wants the children to think about and keep in mind). Children explore and learn about the central concept through a series of related learning *experiences*. Some of the scientific concepts that can be explored in PrePS classrooms are change and transformation, form and function, the distinction between animate and inanimate objects, and systems and interactions. Because these concepts are very broad and can lead a class in many directions, teachers often choose to study a subcategory or aspect of a central concept. For example, a teacher focusing on change and transformation can choose a specific type of change to explore: growth and metamorphosis, seasonal changes, or changes in substance and matter (e.g., liquids and solids). Each of these topics can, in turn, be studied through various areas of inquiry. Learning about changes through growth and metamorphosis, for example, could include areas of inquiry such as the transformations of caterpillars to butterflies; seeds to plants and back to seeds; and babies to children. We call these areas of inquiry *focuses*. Focuses in PrePS are somewhat similar to the themes that are part of many preschool curricula (e.g., the human body, pets, Fall). However, in PrePS, the teacher connects these focuses across the school year with each other and through the underlying central concept. Under this approach, autumn (for example) is not the topic that comes after transportation and before Thanksgiving; it is part of a larger exploration and links to learning opportunities that have come before and to ones the teacher has planned for the future.

Once the teacher chooses a central concept for PrePS, goals for learning and exploration can be defined. These learning goals *bridge* the content children will be exploring. Consider the concept of *growth*. A teacher may set a main goal for children to discover either 1) what living things need to grow or 2) how plant and animal life cycles are similar. In learning about the concept of seasonal changes, the bridge might be for children to think about how seasonal changes affect living things. These conceptual bridges weave throughout planned learning experiences.

For example, the question of what living things need to grow could be explored with experiences that focus on the growth of humans, plants, and animals. Opportunities to explore the focus on plants might include trying to sprout seeds with and without water, growing plants with different amounts of water, trying to grow seeds in different substances (e.g., soil, rocks, sand), and putting potted plants in different parts of the classroom to compare their growth rates by measuring stalks or roots. Note that these experiences introduce simple experiments to examine the effect of light, water, and growing medium on growth outcomes. Similarly, to help children think about how the body changes as humans mature from babies to children to adults, the teacher might include the following activities: measuring body parts like feet or hands; making charts that show how many children have feet that are 5, 6, and 7 inches long; bringing in baby pictures so that children can compare how they looked as an infant with how they look now; and keeping records of changes in shoe or clothing size. These are just a few of the examples of how a teacher might plan to relate different learning opportunities to a central concept. The main point is that a teacher who uses PrePS plans a variety of experiences for each focus. In fact, you might already be thinking about the kinds of related learning experiences that you want to offer your students.

Figure 2.1 illustrates a web of experiences used in PrePS. The central concept is placed in the center of the curriculum plan. This scientific concept is explored through several focuses (plants, humans, and pets) that stem from the central concept *change through growth*. Children are provided with many opportunities to investigate the concept in each of these focus areas. Sets of experiences cluster around each focus, and several focuses stem from the central concept. The learning goal bridges the areas of inquiry. In looking at what living things need to grow, water and nutrients thread through the different focuses in this web of experiences.

As another example, to learn about structures, a class might discuss human bodies, families, and homes (see Figure 2.2). The bridging goal may be to have children explore the importance of the form of these structures for the survival of human species. Although preschoolers cannot grasp all the underlying abstract evolutionary implications, they can participate in activities that explore how shape and structure affect everyday motion and behavior. Daily experiences related to the structure of homes can include the following:

1. Drawing or building a model of one's own home (with parental help)

2. Walking around the school's neighborhood to observe various types of human homes

3. Making graphs of the types of homes in which students live

4. Using group discussions and research, children can compare and contrast their own homes with shelters built by people who live in different climates and environments than their own

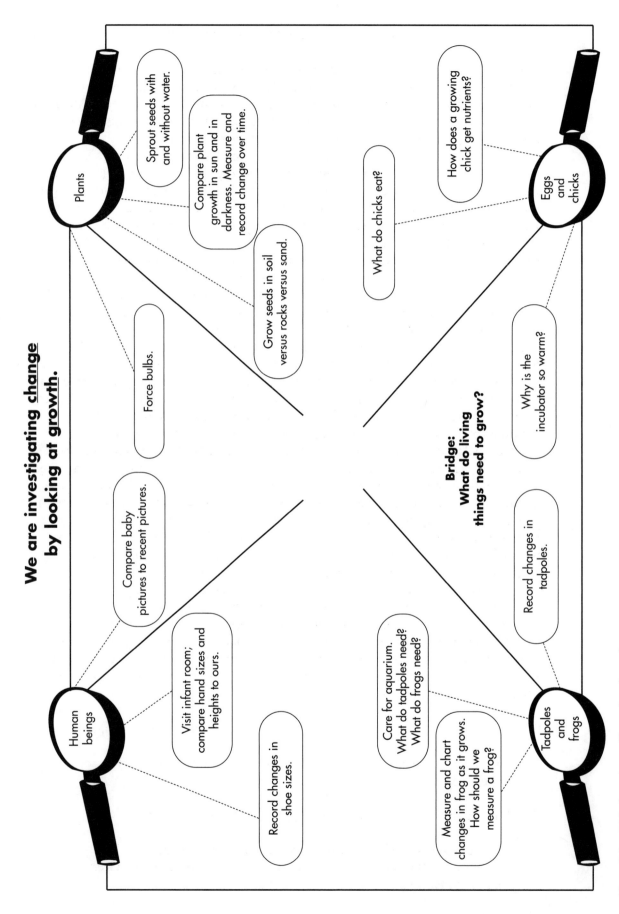

We are investigating change by looking at growth.

Plants
- Sprout seeds with and without water.
- Compare plant growth in sun and in darkness. Measure and record change over time.
- Grow seeds in soil versus rocks versus sand.
- Force bulbs.

Eggs and chicks
- How does a growing chick get nutrients?
- What do chicks eat?
- Why is the incubator so warm?

Human beings
- Compare baby pictures to recent pictures.
- Visit infant room; compare hand sizes and heights to ours.
- Record changes in shoe sizes.

Tadpoles and frogs
- Care for aquarium. What do tadpoles need? What do frogs need?
- Measure and chart changes in frog as it grows. How should we measure a frog?
- Record changes in tadpoles.

Bridge: What do living things need to grow?

Figure 2.1. Web of experiences: Change through growth.

20

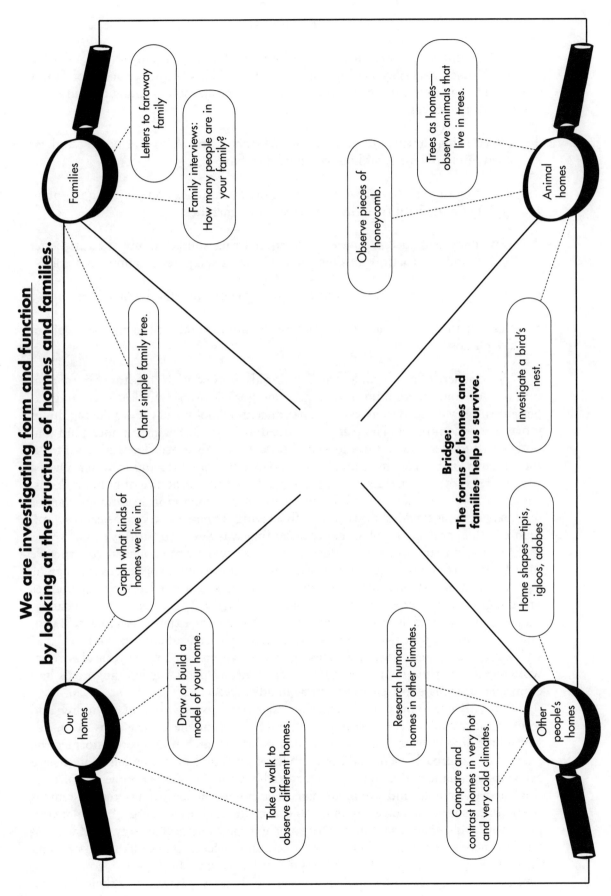

We are investigating form and function by looking at the structure of homes and families.

Families
- Letters to faraway family
- Family interviews: How many people are in your family?
- Chart simple family tree.

Animal homes
- Trees as homes—observe animals that live in trees.
- Observe pieces of honeycomb.
- Investigate a bird's nest.

Our homes
- Graph what kinds of homes we live in.
- Draw or build a model of your home.
- Take a walk to observe different homes.

Bridge: The forms of homes and families help us survive.

Other people's homes
- Home shapes—tipis, igloos, adobes
- Research human homes in other climates.
- Compare and contrast homes in very hot and very cold climates.

Figure 2.2. Web of experiences: Form and function (structure).

21

In the same vein, children could explore why families are important and what role family members play in children's daily lives. The abstract concept of family forms and functions can be illustrated through the following kinds of hands-on, minds-on experiences:

1. Interviewing other children about which family members live nearby and far away, and how many siblings or aunts they have

2. Counting the number of people in each other's families and graphing the number of families with two, three, four, or more members

3. Describing extended families and then charting simple family trees to better understand the relationships between grandparents, parents, aunts, and uncles

4. Writing letters or drawing pictures to mail to extended family members

5. Looking through magazines for pictures of families and making up stories about the photos

The teachers of a class of 4- and 5-year-olds worked with the same central concept of form and function but used a different goal to bridge children's learning experiences. They decided to investigate the concept by looking at the way living things move (i.e., locomotion). The teachers wanted children to begin to understand that body structure determines the way that different animals move. They chose to focus their inquiry on people and animals that move in air, on land, and in water. Over a period of several months, children investigated the body structure of humans, birds, squirrels, fish, and seals to explore the question of locomotion in different species (e.g., having wings makes it possible to fly, having flippers makes it easier to swim). Figure 2.3 illustrates the web of experiences that was designed for this class.

In a given year, most teachers use only one or two central concepts to structure their PrePS curriculum. The number of focuses and learning experiences that can be used to illustrate a given central concept are numerous, and the learning experiences one designs can cut across many curricular areas. Figure 2.4 presents a weekly activities planning sheet that teachers might use to outline the experiences they will provide to support children's learning about a particular central concept and focus, as well as to meet other critical curricular goals. A workable plan for your classroom will emerge from the many possibilities when strong plans for learning goals and connected learning experiences are made in advance.

Table 2.1 lists some central concepts and subcategories with which children and teachers have had success working. Although some of these ideas may seem advanced for preschoolers, keep in mind the kind of research findings that formed the basis of our approach. Many other possibilities exist, and some implicit concepts are even more fundamental than the ones featured in Table 2.1. For example, the distinction between animate and inanimate objects embodies the idea of differential sources of energy to support change. Animate objects create their own energy. Inanimate objects move and change as a function of some external source of energy. Still, we hesitate to encourage the use of *energy* as a central concept because its understanding depends on advanced knowledge of physics and biology. Children who come to appreciate the idea that animate objects move on their own because of their material

We are investigating form and function by looking at the locomotion of living things.

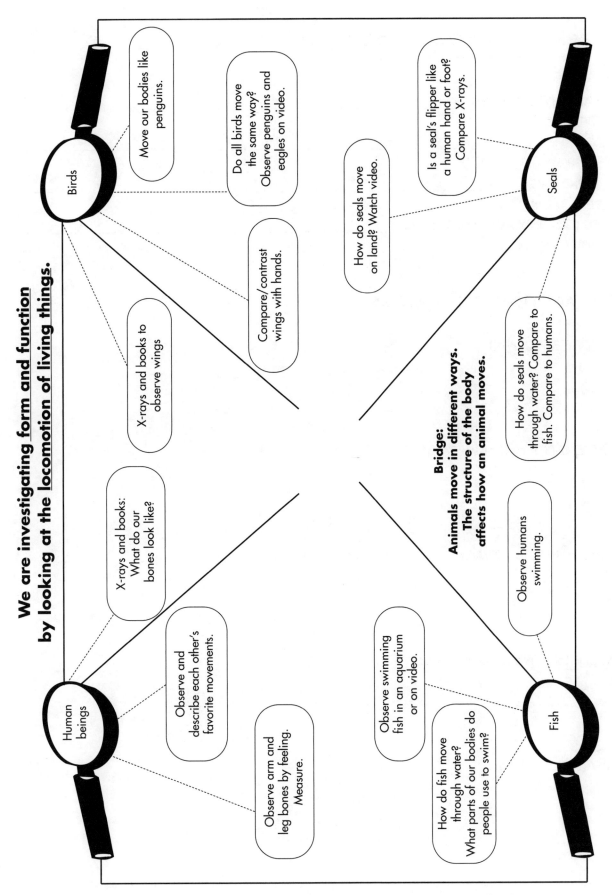

Birds
- Move our bodies like penguins.
- Do all birds move the same way? Observe penguins and eagles on video.
- Compare/contrast wings with hands.
- X-rays and books to observe wings

Seals
- Is a seal's flipper like a human hand or foot? Compare X-rays.
- How do seals move on land? Watch video.
- How do seals move through water? Compare to fish. Compare to humans.

Human beings
- X-rays and books: What do our bones look like?
- Observe and describe each other's favorite movements.
- Observe arm and leg bones by feeling. Measure.

Fish
- Observe swimming fish in an aquarium or on video.
- How do fish move through water? What parts of our bodies do people use to swim?
- Observe humans swimming.

Bridge:
Animals move in different ways. The structure of the body affects how an animal moves.

Figure 2.3. Web of experiences: Form and function (locomotion).

23

Weekly Activities Planning Sheet

WEEK OF
_____

WE ARE INVESTIGATING_____
(Central Concept)

THROUGH_____
(Subcategory)

BY EXPLORING_____
(Focus)

HOW IT IS/THEY ARE AFFECTED BY_____
(Bridge)

OUR ACTIVITIES WILL INCLUDE

SCIENCE EXPLORATION

MATHEMATICS AND NUMERACY

LANGUAGE AND LITERACY

PERCEPTUAL AND SENSORY SKILLS

CREATIVITY

(page 1 of 2)

Figure 2.4.   Weekly activities planning sheet.

(continued)

Weekly Activities Planning Sheet

DRAMATIC PLAY AND IMAGINATION

MUSIC AND MOVEMENT

FINE MOTOR

GROSS MOTOR

OUTSIDE EXPLORATION

SOCIAL-EMOTIONAL

THINGS FROM HOME

Table 2.1.   Examples of possible central concepts and related ideas

Change and transformation	Systems and interactions
Growth and decay	Ecosystems
Seasonal/weather	Symbiotic relationships
Reversible/irreversible	Blood circulation
Substance/matter (e.g., liquid, solid, gas)	Plumbing
Living/nonliving things	Habitats and climates
Animate/inanimate distinction	Form and function
Growth and decay	Animal and human movement
Insides/outsides	Animal and human homes
Movement	Communication
Internal/external locus of control	Tools and their uses

makeup will be on a relevant learning path to learn more about biology when they go on to school. Similarly, children who learn about the conditions of change for inanimate objects will have a relevant knowledge base to learn physics. Teachers can take pleasure from preparing children to be eager to study more science in the future.

In the PrePS program, the teacher's primary role is to guide children as they make discoveries and connections. Remember, what the children are thinking about is almost more important than what they are physically doing. Hands-on activity is critical, but it should be activity with a goal in mind. No day's activities are isolated from those that have come before or those that will follow. Once a teacher becomes comfortable with it, a PrePS lesson plan can lighten the teacher's workload because the day's activities flow together, so it is less important to separate "math time" from "science time" from "reading time." These skills will naturally fit into the activities that the PrePS teacher develops.

When describing PrePS to others, we often contrast the program's definition of science with what we term "birthday party science" or "magic show science." In the latter, an adult creates an exciting visual display while children observe. The audience sits back while the performer mixes, for example, baking soda and vinegar to create something like an exploding volcano. This explosion, while interesting, is not treated as anything more than an exciting parlor trick. The children are not given the opportunity to explore the properties of the powders and liquids being used or to understand what typically happens when wet and dry substances are mixed together. Contrast this with the approach of a PrePS teacher who engaged children in a related experience (see Box 2.1).

PrePS relies on the teacher's own creativity and enthusiasm, to design an individual curriculum plan. We know that presenting children with a list of facts is not the best way to learn science. Nor is it necessary for educators to teach from a fixed set of curriculum units. PrePS provides a flexible curriculum framework for teachers to tailor to their own ideas and goals. We note as well that while teachers should have plans, they also will need to respond to children's desire to take some side trips. Children may have ideas, questions, and interests that lead the class to unanticipated discoveries. But keep in mind the need to return from the side trip to the main pathway.

FLEXIBLE PLANS

In PrePS, teachers carefully plan learning activities, but flexibility is needed to really maximize learning opportunities. The PrePS approach encourages children's active participation in their own learning. They will let you know what they are most in-

Box 2.1
THE PrePS APPROACH TO EXPERIMENTS

A PrePS teacher had this to say about demonstrations of the reaction when baking soda and vinegar are mixed:

> *Well, the baking soda and vinegar experiment doesn't mean anything at all, really, if it's not related to other stuff you're doing in the class. You want to connect the experiment to a more central theme (the overarching central concept).*

This teacher pointed out that before children could begin to understand the baking soda and vinegar display in any meaningful way, they would need to understand that this reaction is not what typically happens when liquids are mixed with powders:

> *If you're exploring the central theme of change for this [experiment], you could explore the change of wet to dry, or the change of solid to liquid.*

The teacher could put out a series of white powders (e.g., corn flour, rice flour, baking powder, sugar, gelatin) for the children to explore in small groups. The children can then systematically compare and contrast the powders using their senses (e.g., touch, smell, sight, even taste) and record their observations with the help of a teacher.

> *See, this way, they're learning vocabulary (e.g., texture, smooth, rough, sweet, sour, wet, dry) and you're giving them words that they can use in other experiences.*

This activity of comparing the white powders ties in conceptually with other activities the class will do—comparing fruits with vegetables, for example, or discussing how the skin on fingertips perceives textures.

As explained by this teacher, the class might never actually get to the formal procedure of adding 3 drops of vinegar to 5 tablespoons of baking soda to produce a reaction. The PrePS approach emphasizes sound investigative methods over specific activities or reactions. In this classroom, the children learned in a hands-on, small-group context to think about taste and texture variations among powders, which initially looked almost identical. Using appropriate vocabulary and thinking in organized, critical ways is much more valuable to learners than witnessing a single, inexplicable reaction.

Once children realize that not all white powder is created equal, they are better able to predict that adding water to each could affect the powders in different ways. One class conducted a series of experiments in which they cooked white rice in different liquids: water, apple juice, lemon juice, milk, and chocolate milk; they predicted how each liquid would affect the color and taste of rice. Then each child tried a bite of the cooked rice and, with the help of an adult, recorded observations of the finished product. The concrete activity remained the same—combining rice and liquid over heat—but the children had to consider what they knew about each type of liquid, and so treated each trial as a separate case. Predictions and observations were written down so that children could check their expectations against actual results. Notice that language and literacy skills are emphasized here, along with the science and math skills needed to explore common liquids and to follow a recipe. Children's predictions about cooking rice in hot chocolate tell us that they have reasonable ideas about what might occur. For example, one girl predicted:

> *The rice . . . will taste sour . . . be yellow, and it will burn.*

terested in, and they will lead you onto new paths with their questions and ideas. Although you will be able to anticipate some of these detours, you will be surprised and impressed by others. Learning truly is a collaboration between teacher and learner. You should not be afraid to add new activities or even new focuses that reflect student interests, but do keep in mind the need to have connections between these new activities and others that are planned. Box 2.2 illustrates this balance between planning and flexibility.

The interplay between the teacher's plans and the students' interests has a number of subtle implications that often go unrecognized or underappreciated. By responding to children's questions and interests with new activities, the teacher is showing the students that their thoughts are valuable and powerful. Children are proud and excited that they are contributing to their own learning. In some cases, the children's questions may be so powerful that the teacher does not know the answer. By saying, "I don't know. Let's find out together," the teacher shows children that having all the answers is less important than knowing how to get them. Children's questions might also reveal that they have not interpreted information in the way teachers intended; some misinterpretations likely will occur as a result of the children's efforts to assimilate new ideas. When this happens, provide learning experiences that guide children to more accurate understandings. This assimilation process

---

Box 2.2
FLEXIBILITY AND PrePS

At one point in the year, a preschool class was investigating the central concept of insides and outsides. Most of the class's activities involved two focuses: 1) fruits and vegetables and 2) the body. During one of the activities about fruits and vegetables, children began to wonder what happens to food inside their bodies. A number of activities grew from this question. Children used stethoscopes to listen to food being chewed and swallowed, and they listened to their stomach sounds as digestion occurred.

Discussion of body parts such as the stomach and esophagus led to questions about bones, so the next activity involved bones and joints. Specifically, finger splints and temporary casts were used to immobilize certain joints. Children then attempted to use those joints (e.g., trying to pick up coins with their thumbs taped against their hands). The topic of bones was expanded to include dinosaurs and fossils. The teacher could not provide hands-on, small-group activities with real dinosaur artifacts, so the teacher thought about other ways to learn about bones and decided to use a fish. First, children made prints of the outside of a fish's body. Then they used a clean fish skeleton to make their own fossil by pressing the skeleton into plaster. (*Note:* The teacher cooked the fish so that it was not wasted. Here, as elsewhere when we use food, we eat it when it is practical and sanitary to do so.)

By responding to the new directions that children wanted to explore, this teacher was able to prepare follow-up activities that enabled children to answer questions that interested them. At the same time, the teacher was able to keep the children on the planned learning pathway—thinking about the insides and outsides of humans and other living things.

will take time, but children will work through tremendous amounts of information if given the time to explore in their own ways. Although the quick route is to provide direct answers and solutions, deeper understanding results when children make discoveries and connections for themselves. Providing multiple opportunities to explore the same concept is one critical ingredient for deeper understanding.

CONCLUSION

PrePS is an approach for introducing science to preschoolers. As such, it lays out some clear guidelines that must be followed (e.g., learning experiences should cohere around a central concept), but the exact details of how your plans unfold will vary from class to class. This is one reason we use the term *pathways* to describe our approach. Imagine you are a guide at the Grand Canyon. Your goal is to get your group to the canyon, but the specific path you take to get to your destination can vary. As the guide, you have carefully planned the path you will take, but you also know that the trip can be enhanced for your tour group by exploring a side path or stopping to investigate an interesting plant they ask you about. The guide gets the group to the end goal but remains flexible because there is more than one path to take to arrive at that goal. As one PrePS teacher put it:

> [The children] will tell you what they want to do along the way. They'll let you know what they're interested in, and they'll ask questions you never even thought about. Don't be afraid to stop and investigate, but don't let them take over the whole trip. Set goals. When you start a new project, what do you want the kids to be thinking about?

The remainder of this book will facilitate your transition to PrePS.

3

Key Science Practices

Science content and science practices naturally and necessarily go together (Kuhn, 1962). Engaging in science practices (e.g., observing and predicting) requires content (something to observe and learn more about). In Chapter 2, we concluded that certain content areas are more appropriate for early education because they are built on competences that preschoolers already have. Conceptual content is also more powerful when children have the opportunity to explore it fully over time rather than moving from one idea to another. In these ways, content matters, but teaching children content without having them engage in science practices makes science seem like a list of facts. It also encourages the idea that science is something that *other* people do and think about. Our goal in Preschool Pathways to Science (PrePS™) is to encourage the scientist-in-waiting in all children by allowing them to wonder, explore, and investigate big ideas. This chapter focuses on science practices, while fully acknowledging the critical interdependence of these practices with science content.

Children in the PrePS program are encouraged to think, talk, and work scientifically. These practices go together—you cannot have one without the others. Children who are actively observing, predicting, and checking are also learning the correct vocabulary words to describe these actions. They think differently about an item that they are observing rather than just glancing at it. More specifically, we have chosen to focus on five key science practices that we use to describe ways of thinking and doing science. Each practice is presented as a group of related skills:

1. Observe, predict, check

2. Compare, contrast, experiment

3. Vocabulary, discourse, and language

4. Counting, measurement, and math

5. Recording and documenting

Throughout this chapter, we illustrate these key science practices using content from various conceptual domains. This approach provides more examples of learning experiences found in PrePS classrooms. It also shows how the science practices can be applied across a relatively broad range of content. We begin with our approach for introducing a class to observing, predicting, and checking; however, these examples also involve many other science practices. Science practices are difficult to consider in isolation because most science learning activities incorporate more than one of them.

OBSERVE, PREDICT, CHECK

For many years, we have introduced the idea of *observation* using an apple. The activity occurs during group time, with the teacher either providing an apple for each child or passing around one apple. As the fruit is passed, each child makes an observation (e.g., "It looks red," "It smells sweet," "It feels cold"). These observations are written down by the teacher, aide, or another adult. Note that in these early attempts, participation is more important than accuracy. For example, if a child says, "The apple smells juicy," the teacher should not correct that statement. Instead, the teacher should ask what the child means by asking, "It smells juicy? What does juice smell like?" Other children might hold the apple up to their ears, observing that it does not make noise.

This example may sound unrealistic. After all, most preschoolers are very familiar with apples, so how can a teacher possibly expect to hold their attention with them? However, this is one of the amazing things about doing science with young children—it allows everyone involved to consider common, everyday objects and occurrences in fresh ways. Video of a new class observing an apple for the first time is striking because the children attend so carefully to the task. One teacher who watched such a tape remarked that the children acted as if they had never seen an apple before. Of course they had seen apples before, but they had not *observed* them. The introduction of a new science term and practice transformed a familiar apple into an object for scientific exploration. Activity 3.1 provides a more detailed description of how observation can be introduced using an apple, and Activity 3.2 describes a simple prediction activity using an apple.

Observing, predicting, and checking are used repeatedly throughout PrePS, even in situations that might not be thought of as science. For example, children can be asked to observe what they see on a book's cover to predict what the story inside will be about. Reading the book is a way to check predictions, encourage literacy, and have fun. When reading a story with new vocabulary, children might be asked to use the story's context to makes guesses about the meaning of new words. Ask children how they can check and find out for sure. They might suggest the teacher use the dictionary or ask another adult. A teacher who is pleased with children's behavior might ask them to observe the teacher's smiling face and to predict how the teacher feels inside. The teacher's happiness is not just a given in this context, but something children can discover using their scientific skills. As the examples in Boxes 3.1 and 3.2 demonstrate, when children are given multiple opportunities to engage in science practices, they integrate new ideas, words, and science practices into their speech and behavior.

Our next step after completing the apple experiences has varied depending on the learning goals of a particular teacher or the interests of the class. Sometimes we continue practicing the observe-predict-check sequence using different fruits and vegetables. This also allows us to introduce *comparing and contrasting*. Finding

---

Box 3.1
OBSERVING BIRDS

Children who observed the outside of three birds noted that

- They had black tails with white dots

- They were flying and jumping around

- They had sharp, orange beaks

- They were eating and drinking

- The male and female looked different

- The baby had an orange beak

- They were making peeping sounds

When told they were going to predict what was inside the bird, one child suggested, "Sometimes your own body can give a clue also." This statement is worth thinking about. It shows that the boy understands that human beings and birds share some critical characteristics. It also reveals awareness that, even though a prediction is like a guess, you can use information you already know to help make your guess a good one.

---

seeds in some items but not others can lead into an exploration of plants and the form and function of their parts or discussions of how the insides of fruits differ from their outsides. It could also lead to a discussion of seeds, planting, and growth. Other times, we move into an in-depth exploration of senses (see Chapter 4).

Practice making observations also lends itself well to the introduction and use of certain science tools. Magnifiers work with our sense of vision to allow us to observe objects and details that are too small to see well without magnification. Balance scales can be introduced as tools that help us tell which of two things is heavier, which is especially useful when we are not able to tell just by using our muscles (see Box 3.3). Standards for early education emphasize that young children be exposed to tools that allow them to observe and measure various phenomena. Through PrePS learning experiences, children use observation and measurement tools in a varied and purposeful way, gaining valuable experience not only with the intended use of these tools, but also with the problems to which they can be applied.

COMPARE, CONTRAST, EXPERIMENT

Children quickly become used to making observations by describing objects and events. This ability leads naturally into comparing and contrasting the characteristics of the objects or events observed with those already known. For example, a child might say that mint-scented playdough smells "like toothpaste" or "like gum." Two seashells are both brown, but "one has spots and the other one does not." As chil-

---

Box 3.2
USING PREVIOUS EXPERIENCE TO MAKE PREDICTIONS

One teacher introduced her class to making and testing predictions by asking children to predict how many seeds were in an apple and then cutting the apple open to test the predictions. The class did this every day for a week. The predictions, shaped by experience, became more reasonable and children became more patient listening to others and not rushing to "correct" them. The next week, the teacher was with a 4-year-old child from the class. As she prepared to cut an apple for lunch, the teacher predicted the number of seeds.

Teacher: I predict eight seeds.

Child: Predict five.

Teacher: Nope, I predict eight.

Child: If you want to be more right, say five.

Teacher: I thought we discussed that I can have a different . . .

Child: I know you can have a different prediction than me, and that's ok, but if you want to be right most times, you should say five. Because if you cut the apple in half [crosswise], there's a star kind of thing and each thing [point of star] of it has a seed. So if you want to be right more often, say five.

When the apple was sliced in half, the star shape was revealed. Each point had one seed, and one had an extra. The child's prediction was more accurate than the teacher's and, more important, this prediction was informed by repeated observations and hands-on experience. Children in a PrePS classroom make science words and procedures their own relatively quickly.

---

dren describe items, noticing similarities and differences, they begin to sort and classify them as well.

In our experience, preschoolers have very little difficulty describing the differences between two items. However, they tend to resist agreeing that something about two items is "the same" if the features are not *exactly* the same. For example, most adults would say that a tomato and an apple are the same color, but preschoolers often do not. They may even go so far as to describe one item as being "light red" and the other as "a little bit lighter red" instead of saying that both items are red. We have found it useful to ask children to tell us what is "kind of the same" or "almost the same" instead. We also reframe children's statements in ways that validate their observations of the differences while highlighting a similarity. After the statement above, we said, "Yes, great observation! Both of these things are red. That's something that's kind of the same. But this one is lighter red than that one. That's something that's different."

Box 3.3
INTRODUCING SCIENCE TOOLS

You might already have magnifiers and scales available for your students to use, perhaps in a discovery area or at a science table. While children likely will not learn how to use these tools if they are not in the classroom, the mere presence of these tools does not mean that children will interact with them and figure out how to use them. Classroom observation research shows that children are less inclined to visit science areas than art, dramatic play, and block areas (Gelman Cognitive Development and Learning Lab, unpublished data). Furthermore, when they are in the science area, children often do not use the tools and materials in the intended way. Children should be given time to explore science tools on their own, but they also need guidance from teachers on the ways that the tools help us observe and measure the world.

To introduce magnifiers, for example, you can set up a situation in which students need to see details on an object more closely than they can with just their eyes. Counting the legs on an insect, observing the patterns of a fingerprint, or observing the rings on a slice of tree trunk are easier when magnifiers are used. You can let children know that they still need their eyes to see, but the magnifier and their eyes work together, as a team, to allow them to see some things better (see Figure 3.1). The magnifier helps them to *observe*.

Figure 3.1. Using a magnifying glass.

Figure 3.2. Using the balance scale.

The balance scale (see Figure 3.2) can be introduced by building on children's knowledge that they can use their muscles to tell which of two objects is heavier. In a situation in which two items weigh almost the same, using muscles and feeling weight will not tell the children which item is heavier. As they learned with magnifiers, sometimes their senses need help. A balance scale helps students find out which of two objects (or sets of them) weighs more or whether their weights are equal. Introducing children to science tools in a meaningful way increases their tendency to go to a science area to explore that tool, and other materials, on their own (Nayfeld, Brenneman, & Gelman, 2009).

When we change the task a bit, children show that they know both the tomato and apple are red. If the adult provides the category for children and asks them to sort items (e.g., "Put the red things together"), children are quite good at doing so. Similarly, when told that we might go on a picnic and want to take red foods along, they have no trouble listing tomato, apple, watermelon, and so on (Macario, 1991). Children can practice sorting using shells, pebbles, or nuts, which can be grouped by size, color, and shape. Sorting natural objects with natural variability helps children to ignore irrelevant differences and focus on the factors that lead objects to belong to a common category. Such a sorting task allows children to practice the thinking skills necessary to go beyond identical similarity to identify less obvious common features.

The ability to identify similarities and differences is a critical thinking skill that applies across many content domains including literature, science, and math. This skill eventually expands when children begin to categorize objects or events by privileging some similar relations or attributes over others (Gentner, 2005). For example, a child will come to understand that the physical similarities between whales and fish are less important biologically than the way whales breathe and give birth. Research completed by Susan Gelman and Ellen Markman (among others) suggests that even very young children can go beyond similar looks to properly classify animals based on deeper, more abstract similarities. Gelman and Markman (1986) showed preschoolers three pictures at a time: a flamingo, a bat, and a blackbird. Two were from the same category (birds: flamingo and blackbird) and two looked alike (blackbird and bat). Children were told, "This bird (flamingo) gives its baby mashed-up food, and the bat gives its baby milk" and then were asked what the blackbird fed its baby. If preschoolers were led astray by similarity of looks, they should have answered, "Milk." Most of the time, however, they used the species of the animal, not what it looked like, to make their decisions. We have offered PrePS learning activities that build on this competence. One activity involved identifying similarities and differences among snakes, eels, and fish after children learned that eels are fish rather than snakes. The importance of the activity is not just to learn that fact, though. It is to highlight that one can gather evidence to support a conclusion and that some similarities matter more than others when thinking about categories of animals—or anything else.

The ability to compare and contrast is also a foundation for understanding experimentation. In its simplest form, a true experiment involves two objects or events that differ in only one way. The objects are treated in the same manner, and differences in outcome are compared. When a difference in outcome occurs, we can say that the one critical difference between the two items was related to the difference in outcomes. (We are glossing over some of the complexities here, of course, but this is the logic of a simple experiment.) As an example, imagine you have heard that lemon juice will keep cut apples from turning brown. To test this idea in a simple experiment, you would cut an apple, brush one half with lemon juice and leave the other half alone. Observed differences between the two can then be attributed to the lemon juice because that was the only variable that differed between the two apple halves. If, instead, you cut both a Granny Smith and a Red Delicious apple in half and put lemon juice on the Granny Smith only and observe that the Red Delicious turned brown but the other apple did not, you cannot be sure that it was the lemon juice, rather than the variety of apple, that contributed to the difference in outcome. Children in a PrePS classroom are given multiple opportunities to experiment in both the common and scientific senses of the term.

In PrePS, teachers do not spend a lot of time explaining logic; they just engage in simple, controlled experiments so that children have experiences doing so. Teachers frame a question, often drawn from children's own questions. The class then uses the experimental method to try to find out the answer. These investigations relate to the concept the class is exploring, and often, children already know something relevant to the investigation. For example, a number of preschoolers can say that plants need sun to grow. Consider turning this into an experiment by growing the same kind of plant in a closet and near the window. This simple experiment provides firsthand experience that allows children to gather their own evidence (see Box 3.4). In this way, a science fact can become something children understand, rather than just something they can say. Simple experiments also give children the opportunity to experience one of the important ways that knowledge is built in science. Scientists explore, investigate, and experiment to establish understandings. One goal of PrePS is that children will come to view scientific methods as important means of gathering information to explore the questions they have about the world.

VOCABULARY, DISCOURSE, AND LANGUAGE

Children should be given the chance to learn the appropriate scientific words that go along with their investigations. Science vocabulary allows children to discuss their discoveries and questions in deeper, richer ways than are possible with everyday language. At first, it may seem unrealistic to expect a 4-year-old child to use and understand words like *observe* and *research*, but young children acquire vocabulary rapidly (see Chapter 2). Preschoolers can learn to use these terms when they are used repeatedly and in appropriate contexts. Children are naturally inclined to observe, explore, and investigate the world. When teachers provide words for these processes, their importance is highlighted. Children who engage in these processes also begin to reflect on what they are doing and to think and talk about their explorations.

Terms that describe science practices (e.g., *observe, predict, record, journal, compare, contrast*) can be introduced indirectly or directly by teachers. A teacher can say, "I observe that it is raining outside" instead of "It's raining." Children should not be expected to immediately grasp these new words. However, because the science practice terms are used over and over, along with the practices themselves, children are given repeated exposure to science vocabulary in various contexts which supports learning with meaning. Teachers also can introduce nouns and adjectives relevant to the specific content being explored. If the lesson is about plants, teachers can use words to label the parts (e.g., *roots, stem, leaves, seeds, flowers*), name the specific plants being studied (e.g., *beans, marigolds, cactuses*), and describe their attributes (e.g., *long, thin, yellow, prickly*). Because PrePS explores similar content over a long period of time, children have the opportunity to encounter new words multiple times in different contexts, thus making it more likely that children will learn them with understanding.

We do have some cautions for vocabulary use. If you are planning to introduce a new term, think carefully about how you will explain it to preschoolers in an accurate and appropriate way. David Hammer (1999), a physics and education professor, warned against possible problems of using scientific terms that refer to complicated notions to replace children's intuitive understandings of science phenomena.

Box 3.4
SIMPLE EXPERIMENTS

As part of an exploration of seasonal changes with a focus on animal adaptations to winter and cold, we did experiments to explore the insulation properties of blubber, feathers, and other materials. The experiments involved filling double-layered, sealed plastic bags with "blubber" (solid vegetable shortening). Children slid one hand into a glove filled with blubber and one into glove without blubber. Then they dunked their hands into a bucket of icy water (see Figure 3.3).

　　(Note that we used the exact same glove without filling for the control in this experiment. If the children just put their bare hands in the ice water, there would be a confound in the experiment: There would be no way to be sure that it was the filling, rather than the glove itself, that was insulating the hand. The children probably will not think about this problem with the experiment, but you will know that you have exposed them to a fair test of the question.)

　　Prior to the procedure, children were asked to predict whether blubber or no blubber will keep their hands warmer. After the experiment, children recorded their findings on a results chart. We extended the learning and the opportunity to practice proper experimental procedures by varying the substances in the gloves (feathers versus no feathers and blubber versus feathers). This series of explorations took place over a number of days using different glove combinations. We found that after having this sort of extended experience (compared with not having it), children become better at designing their own simple experiments to answer "find-out" questions. This is an important foundation for the lessons they will encounter in school science.

　　See Activity 3.3 for a more detailed description of how to set up this experiment.

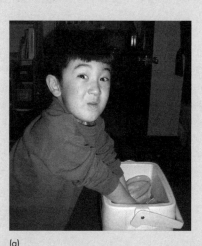

(a)

(b)

Figure 3.3.　Blubber glove experiment (a) and results chart (b). The results chart reads: "Does Blubber or Feathers keep hands warmer?" Children wrote their names under either the Feathers column (left side of chart) or the Blubber column (right side of chart).

Table 3.1. Words to use again and again

Observe	Senses	Describe	Investigate	Shape	Count	Record
Observation	See	Compare	Investigation	Size	Measure	Journal
Predict	Touch	Contrast	Explore	Height	Measurement	
Prediction	Texture	Same	Discover	Length		
Check	Hear	Different	Experiment	Width		
Findings	Smell	Similarities	Test	Weigh		
Results	Taste	Differences		Weight		

He related the example of a science magician who showed 5-year-old children that he could not push a water-filled balloon into a beaker because the air in the beaker got in the way. He asked children what to do and the suggestion was made to "get the air out." The scientist replied, "Close. We have to use *energy*." Hammer contended that the 5-year-old child's explanation made more sense than the scientist's—and surely, it made more sense to the other children. Words are critical tools for children to express their scientific understandings and ideas. Listen to children's explanations not for the presence of "big" science terms, but for understanding (Appelbaum & Clark, 2001; Gallas, 1995). Children should feel comfortable with and confident about science. To best support and extend children's science understandings and language, teachers should choose their words carefully—and then use them often (see Table 3.1).

Practicing science encourages the use of descriptive language as one observes, compares, and contrasts features of objects and events in the world. Discussing the methods and conceptual content of science requires the use of complex sentences that include embedded clauses and prepositional phrases. For example, one can use a simple sentence to say, "Plants grow." However, to talk about what plants need to grow or how they grow, the sentences become more complex, such as "If you water a plant, it can grow," or "Plants need sun and soil to grow." As conceptual understandings become more detailed, so does the language required to represent them accurately (Gelman & Brenneman, in press; Gelman, Romo & Francis, 2002). As children's scientific and linguistic skills grow, the two mutually reinforce each other, with each becoming more complex. The excerpts in Box 3.5 from group discussions illustrate our point.

COUNTING, MEASUREMENT, AND MATH

In general, very little math is taught in preschool classrooms (Ginsburg, Lee, & Boyd, 2008). What little does occur often focuses on worksheets in which children match pictures of groups of items to numerals that represent the set size (Stipek, 2008). Using and supporting mathematical thinking skills in the context of science allows teachers to bring more meaningful mathematics into the classroom. It also allows children to use skills other than rote counting. PrePS encourages mathematical thinking by providing opportunities for children to use math as a tool for defining and describing the world. These opportunities are not separate from ongoing activities. Because math is used with purpose as part of science experiences, it often generates surprisingly sophisticated thinking from young children. As an illustration, consider Activity 3.2. Each day, children made predictions about the number of seeds in an

Box 3.5
USING SCIENCE VOCABULARY

These transcripts come from two classes, one that serves a predominantly immigrant Spanish-speaking neighborhood and one that serves a university community. As part of an activity series exploring the differences between animate and inanimate objects (see related material in Chapters 1 and 2), we read and discussed Leo Lionni's *Alexander and the Wind-Up Mouse* (2006, Knopf Books for Young Readers). The story describes the interactions between two mice: Alexander, who is real, and Willy, who is a wind-up toy. Notice children's use of complex sentences and their use of descriptive vocabulary. The examples also illustrate how much children know about the needs and abilities of real versus toy animals and demonstrate some sophisticated socioemotional awareness.

Teacher:	[Tell me] one reason why you think this one is Alexander and this one is Willy. This one is real and this one is not. What is your reason?
Child:	Because that one has a wind thingy to wind it up and that one doesn't.
Teacher:	That is an excellent reason.
Child:	And that one has wheels, and that one doesn't.
Teacher:	That is also . . .
Child:	And that one has legs.

Teacher:	Okay, the key for the door, you put it in and turn it, and this is the key on a mouse, you also turn it.
Child:	Yeah, and it goes away with the wheels.
Teacher:	And it goes away with the wheels.
Child:	Yeah.
Teacher:	Do you need to turn this one (real mouse) to make it go around?
Children:	No!
Child:	It just moves by itself.
Teacher:	It just moves by itself.
Children:	Because it's real! Because it has legs!

Teacher:	What does [Alexander] want in the kitchen?
Children:	Crumbs.
Teacher:	Crumbs of what?
Child:	Cheese.
Other child:	Food.
Teacher:	Cheese, food. Do you think Willy needs to get food?
Children:	No.

Teacher:	Do you think Willy *can* get food?
Children:	No.
Child:	He can't open his mouth.
Other child:	Someone would need to wind him up.

Child:	If you step on the mouse, he'll be dead.
Teacher:	It might be dead if you stepped on it? Or hurt?
Child:	Uh-huh.
Teacher:	What happens to a wind up mouse if you step on it?
Child:	It will break.
Teacher:	It will break.
Child:	Because it's a toy.

Child:	He's tired.
Teacher:	He does look tired, why do you say that?
Child:	Because his eyes were almost closed.
Teacher:	Almost closed. The story says that Alexander thought of Willy with *envy*. Hmmm, what would that mean? Alexander longs to be a wind-up mouse like Willy, and be hugged and loved. So envy means he's *jealous*. Means he wishes like he were like Willy.
Child:	Why?
Teacher:	Why does he want to be like Willy? That's a very good question.
Child:	Because he wants everyone to like him like Willy.
Teacher:	I think you're right. I think you're absolutely right.

Child:	The people built the pretend mouse.
Teacher:	People built the pretend mouse? That's a very interesting comment. I don't think we talked about the fact that this one people build. How do we get real mice? Where do they come from?
Children:	Their holes. Their houses.
Teacher:	From their houses?
Child:	They live in the dirt.
Other child:	No, they don't. They live in holes in houses.
Teacher:	But if this one is made by people, what makes a real mouse?
Child:	A mommy!
Teacher:	Ahh, a mommy mouse.

See Activity 3.4 for a science planning grid that relates to this activity and to an extension in which children explore the insides of an actual wind-up toy.

apple, then used counting as a tool to check their ideas. Estimation skills improved as children had repeated opportunities to predict and check the number of seeds found on each day. When children first engage in such activities, estimates may be fantastically large (e.g., "a hundred"), but with relevant experience, they tend to become more realistic and accurate (e.g., "six").

Children's estimation and prediction skills can be harnessed to explore and support their arithmetic capabilities. In one PrePS classroom, the teacher, Susan Wood, sang a song with children in which a baker had nine donuts (represented on a flannel board): "Along came John with one penny to pay. He got one donut and walked away." A designated child removed one donut, and the class was responsible for predicting the remaining number. Ideas tended to vary, but most were reasonable and in the right direction (e.g., "Maybe seven," "I think eight"). Predictions were checked by counting. The song worked so well to elicit mathematical reasoning that researcher Osnat Zur and Wood tried a version that involved taking two or three items away and then adding back these values. Even with this more difficult numerical task, children caught on quickly. This led to the development of a task that systematically explored children's addition, subtraction, and counting skills in a series of research studies (Zur & Gelman, 2004). In this activity, counting was not rote; it was related to the goal of doing arithmetic and checking arithmetic predictions.

In another classroom, the teachers explored a papaya as part of an investigation about the kinds of things that have seeds inside. Most of the children had never seen a papaya (see Figure 3.4), so the teachers engaged children in an observe-predict-check exploration with this novel object. When it was cut open to check the predictions, the class was amazed at the number of seeds. They quickly began shouting estimates of how many there were. The classroom teacher took the chance to acknowledge the children's interest and enthusiasm and to build in an informal mathematics experience. She led them through counting all of the seeds in half of the papaya, then introduced the idea of doubling that number to get a good estimate of the number of seeds in the whole papaya. This experience was so much richer than simply rote counting to large numbers (something seen in preschool classrooms) because it required coordinating a counting procedure that corresponded to actual objects. It also involved doing so with large numbers, giving children experience counting and using large numbers with meaning. Finally, this experience allowed children to put mathematics into action to answer a question that mattered to them, showing that math is a useful tool for solving everyday problems.

Figure 3.4. How many seeds are inside a papaya?

Sorting activities also support children's observation and categorization skills. In one exploration of shells, children sorted shells by size, then again using color. After sorting the shells by color, children counted the number of black, tan, white, and pink shells and made a simple graph of the results. The graph was used to practice comparing quantities (e.g., Are there more white shells or tan shells? Which kind of shell do we have the most of? The fewest?) Discussing quantities using the graph allowed teachers to uncover a really wonderful example of children's mathematical thinking. One boy noted that the shortest bar on the graph was "like a house," the middle bars were "like churches with steeples," and the tallest bar was "a skyscraper." He noticed an ordered pattern of sizes, then generated an analogy. The rea-

Figure 3.5. More activities that incorporate math.

soning displayed was wonderful and reminded us of similar examples when children accurately sort small, medium, and large pinecones as babies, mommies, and daddies. Our point is not that *every* child will show this level of reasoning skill if you incorporate more math into your classroom, but that if you do not incorporate math, you will never know whether children can reason in this way. Further, you will not give them experiences that help them learn to do so and opportunities to talk about their mathematical thinking.

Science activities also provide reasons to use measurement tools (see Figure 3.5). If rulers and scales are simply placed on a science table, children may not grasp that these tools provide organized ways to describe the world. As described earlier, the introduction of a tool as part of an ongoing activity increases the chance that children will use measuring tools in a productive, motivated way. Of course, a child who prefers to use a wooden ruler as a sword is not going to change behavior overnight. Independent exploration of tools allows children to use their creativity; guided exploration helps children understand how the tool can help them learn and allows for more purposeful independent exploration in the future. By including carefully chosen observation and measurement tools in the environment and providing examples of how to use them, a teacher allows children to become familiar with them, to explore the jobs they do, and to consider everyday activities in new ways (see Box 3.6).

By providing opportunities for children to use mathematics in concrete and meaningful ways (e.g., measuring a block tower, comparing their heights to those of friends, tracking changes in the height of sunflower plants over time), PrePS encourages mathematical awareness and confidence. Math is embraced as a useful tool for discovery before the first elementary school textbook is opened. We hope, too, that these early experiences provide a gentle introduction to a lifetime of mathematics learning. If children believe that they can do math and that it is useful and interesting, they are less likely to be afraid of or dislike it as they grow older.

> ### Box 3.6
> ## USING OBSERVATION AND MEASUREMENT TOOLS
>
> One example of a new perspective on everyday activities comes from children we worked with at the Douglass Psychology Child Study Center at Rutgers University. As part of an exploration about snakes, children were learning about the different ways that snakes kill their prey. The book we used to find out about this also described the average length of each snake. We found out that the reticulated python is 32 feet long.
>
> As a way to make this number more real to children, two of us decided to take the class outside and measure out 32 feet. At first, we measured using rulers and a tape measure, but this really was not of much interest to kids. Once we had marked off 32 feet, we decided to have children lay down head-to-toe to measure the same length as the snake. The class found out that the reticulated python is 9 kids long—and we found out that the traditional measuring tool was not of great interest until it was linked to a more familiar unit—real kids!
>
> When we went inside, the children themselves extended this exploration and practiced using their new ideas about measurement. Armed with their knowledge that an indigo snake is 8 feet long, a tape measure, and Lincoln Logs, a few children decided to find out how many Lincoln Logs long the indigo snake would be. The teacher used the tape measure to measure 8 feet, locked it, and the children lined the logs on top of it. In this way, math did not replace free play; rather, it enhanced play, providing another powerful illustration of the ways in which math and science are part of everyday life.

RECORDING AND DOCUMENTING

A number of the mathematical activities described in the previous section involved recording count data and making simple graphs. The observe-predict-check charts (e.g., Activities 3.1 and 3.2) are also examples of documentation in the preschool classroom. PrePS activities support literacy skills as well as science and math skills. In fact, education researchers at the University of Rochester have developed a successful language and literacy program centered around science because it provides such rich content for discussion (Conezio & French, 2002; French, 2004); science is something to read and write about.

Using Books in the PrePS Classroom

The written word is already part of every preschool classroom, and using storybooks to teach is nothing new. PrePS teachers use nonfiction children's books and science magazines as resources for investigating questions, to research children's questions and predictions, and to find materials and resources for themselves (see Box 3.7 for just a few examples). Additionally, many familiar preschool stories address science themes (see Box 3.8). For example, Lily Toy Hong's *The Empress and the Silkworm*

Box 3.7
NONFICTION BOOKS AND MAGAZINES

Books

Brady, I. (1993). *Wild mouse*. London: Cassell.

Butterfield, M. (1992). *Frog (nature chains)*. New York: Little Simon.

De Bourgoing, P. (1991). *Fruit (Scholastic discovery series)*. New York: Scholastic.

De Bourgoing, P. (1994). *Vegetables in the garden (Scholastic discovery series)*. New York: Scholastic.

Dietl, U. (1995). *The plant-and-grow project book*. New York: Sterling.

Lehn, B. (1999). *What is a scientist?* New York: Millbrook.

Llewellyn, C. (2002). *Slugs and snails (minibeasts)*. New York: Franklin Watts.

Maass, R. (1992). *When autumn comes*. New York: Henry Holt and Co.

Merrill, C. (1990). *A seed is a promise*. New York: Scholastic.

Miller, J. (1986). *Seasons on the farm*. New York: Scholastic.

Olesen, J. (1986). *Snail (Stopwatch series)*. New York: Silver, Burdett.

Ruiz, A.L. (1995). *Animals on the inside: A book of discovery & learning*. New York: Sterling.

Scholastic First Discovery Books. (2002). New York: Cartwheel Books.

Smithsonian Soundprints Series. (2002). San Diego: Silver Dolphin.

Swanson, D. (2002). *Coyotes in the crosswalk: True tales of animal life in the wilds . . . of the city!* New York: Whitecap Books.

Watts, B. (1986). *Honeybee (Stopwatch series)*. New York: Silver, Burdett.

Magazines

Click. Cricket Magazine Publishing.

Kids Discover. Kids Discover.

Your Big Backyard. National Wildlife Foundation.

(1995) can be read as part of a focus on life cycles under the central concept *change and transformation*. Complementary experiences include raising silkworms, researching the food they eat, recording changes with cameras and by drawing, predicting and charting the number of days until moths emerge, and creating a class book that describes the life cycle of these animals (see Figures 3.6 and 3.7). When included in a series of learning experiences that focus on change, a familiar story becomes another node in a web of connected learning opportunities. By reading such stories actively with children and interspersing questions, teachers support language, literacy, and science learning (see Activity 3.4).

Even stories that do not have overt science content can be used to plan activities that strengthen scientific thinking skills. For example, you might choose different versions of a particular story, such as *Jack and the Beanstalk* or *The Gingerbread Man*. After reading one version several times so that children are familiar with it, read another version. Help children identify ways that the stories are the same and ways that they differ. Comparing and contrasting, noticing differences and evaluating their importance are valuable skills in science and other domains.

Box 3.8
FICTION BOOKS

Seasonal and weather changes

dePaola, T. (1982). *Charlie needs a cloak.* New York: Aladdin Paperbacks.
Ehlert, L. (1991). *Red leaf, yellow leaf.* San Diego: Harcourt Big Books.
Hader, B., & Hader, E. (1993). *The big snow.* New York: Simon & Schuster.
Kelley, M. (1998). *Fall is not easy.* Madison, WI: Zino Press Children's Books.
Krauss, R. (1989). *The happy day.* New York: Harper Trophy.
Sendak, M. (1991). *Chicken soup with rice: A book of months.* New York: HarperTrophy.

Ecosystems

Balian, L. (2005). *Where in the world is Henry?* New York: Star Bright Books.
Burton, V.L. (1978). *The little house.* Boston: Houghton Mifflin.
Dr. Seuss. (1971). *The Lorax.* New York: Random House.
Gackenbach, D. (1996). *Mighty tree.* New York: Voyager Books.
Harrison, D. (1978). *Little turtle's big adventure.* New York: Random House.

Change through growth or metamorphosis

Andersen, H.C. (1999). *The ugly duckling.* New York: HarperCollins.
Carle, E. (2005). *The tiny seed.* New York: Little Simon.
Curry, P. (1978). *The pimpernel seed.* New York: Methuen Young Books.
Dowden, A.O.T. (1972). *Wild green things in the city: A book of weeds.* New York: Crowell.
Ehlert, L. (1991). *Growing vegetable soup.* New York: Harcourt Big Books.
Ehlert, L. (1992). *Planting a rainbow.* New York: Voyager Books.
Ehlert, L. (2001). *Waiting for wings.* New York: Harcourt Children's Books.
Hall, Z. (1996). *The apple pie tree.* New York: Scholastic.
Hall, Z. (1999). *It's pumpkin time!* New York: Scholastic.
Ryder, J. (1996). *Where butterflies grow.* New York: Puffin.
Swope, S. (2004). *Gotta go! Gotta go!* New York: Farrar, Strauss, Giroux.

Animal behavior and homes

Cannon, J. (2007). *Stellaluna.* New York: Red Wagon Books.
Edwards, P.D. (1996). *Some smug slug.* New York: HarperCollins.
Garelick, M. (1970). *Where does the butterfly go when it rains?* New York: Addison-Wesley.
Lionni, L. (1974). *Fish is fish.* New York: Dragonfly Books.
Markes, J. (2006). *Good thing you're not an octopus!* New York: HarperTrophy.
McNulty, F. (1987). *The lady and the spider.* New York: HarperTrophy.
Steig, W. (1992). *Amos & Boris.* New York: Farrar, Straus and Giroux.
Stewart, P. (1999). *A little bit of winter.* New York: HarperCollins.

Animate/inanimate distinction

Lionni, L. (2006). *Alexander and the wind-up mouse.* New York: Knopf Books for Young Readers.
Steig, W. (2005). *Sylvester and the magic pebble.* New York: Simon and Schuster Books for Young Readers.
Wells, R. (1982). *A lion for Lewis.* New York: Dial Press.
Williams, M. (1958). *The velveteen rabbit.* New York: Doubleday.

Figure 3.6. Story time can be about science.

Figure 3.7. Some pages from a silkworm book that children created.

Using Science Journals

Journals are simple but important science tools for scientists. They can be introduced to children as tools for recording ideas and information so that these can be remembered and shared. Each child receives a journal (a spiral notebook or steno pad works well) to personalize the cover. Teachers encourage children to use these journals for science activities and not for other kinds of drawing that might be put in a portfolio or a separate notebook. Journals take advantage of preschoolers' natural inclination toward and skill for drawing and promote its use for a particular purpose. Journal use encourages children to draw in a representational way to convey specific information about an experiment or event. Children are not merely asked to "draw an apple." Rather, they are asked to "draw *this* apple that we cut open today." This directs their attention to a real-world object and requires them to translate what they notice about the object—its color, its shape, its parts—when representing it in a journal drawing.

One trend in PrePS classrooms is that children's drawing quality increases when they are asked to draw what is right in front of them and are encouraged to attend to detail. For example, a child who was learning about cloth and texture with his class wanted to recreate the spiral patterns on a piece of cloth he was observing. Spirals are difficult to draw, so it was no surprise that his early attempts were spiky and unrecognizable. But he was determined to get it right and continued trying until the spirals in his journal looked like the spirals on the cloth. The teacher did not draw the spiral for him or urge him to correct his early tries. He was self-motivated and persisted to create an accurate representation. Another child carefully chose several shades of green along with brown and reddish pencils to record the subtle color differences in a narcissus stem.

Children's attempts to journal should be accepted in a nonjudgmental way. Some children will not enjoy journaling at first or will produce what looks like random scribbling. A teacher certainly can scaffold the recording process with sensitive guidance, keeping in mind that individual children develop at their own pace. Suggestions to find just the right color crayon to draw an object or to describe the shape or parts of an object *before* an entry is completed encourage more detailed observation and more accurate recording (see Figure 3.8). If possible, teachers should ask children to describe their entries. These descriptions often shed light on the children's goals. Consider the child who, when journaling an insect, created an entry that looked like uncontrolled scribbling. When asked to describe what she had drawn, the child replied that she had recorded the path of the bug while it moved—not the insect itself. Often, children will surprise you by paying attention to features that adults overlook (see Figure 3.9). Attention to the process of journaling, not just the final product, is critical to understanding children's goals and ideas. More details on using journals to assess children's understanding of science ideas are provided in Chapter 5.

Teachers encourage children to discuss their journal entries by asking questions such as, "You have a lot to say about that. May I write it next to your drawing?" Writing what children have to say about their drawings illustrates the link between spoken and written language. Children start to make the connection that written text represents what was said or thought by themselves or someone else. In fact, we have found that after a few months of journal use, some start to write for themselves, often asking questions about how to spell words or write letters. PrePS provides children with content that they want to record, both by drawing and writing.

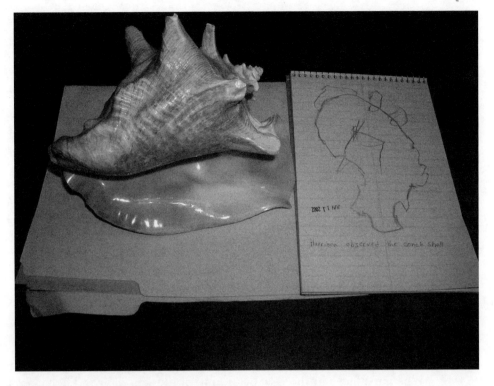

Figure 3.8.   A 3-year-old child's drawing of a conch.

Journals also provide tangible evidence of the passage of time. Teachers can have children use date stamps to mark their journal entries, which initially might seem to be a surprising activity. Many young children do not have an ordered sense of time and calendars, so why use a date stamp? Here the emphasis is on what will develop, not what exists at the beginning of a year. Date stamps can be introduced as a tool to help the class figure out when they did each experiment. By looking at their science journals, children can observe that a seed planted on March 15 sprouted on March 25 and grew to be 1 foot tall on April 27. Date stamps allow children to see where they have been (e.g., "We studied pumpkins back in October") and predict where they are going (e.g., "I bet that flower will be 2 feet tall next week"). Changing the date on the stamps during large group instruction time or at the journal table fosters an awareness of the passage of time and of the stamps' function to record this change. The abstract concept of time is rendered somewhat more concrete. Of course, the date stamps are new and exciting so it takes some time for children to learn to use them properly rather than as decoration (see Figure 3.10). Children might use any blank page to record their observations. The stamped dates mark the entries; therefore, the order is not lost.

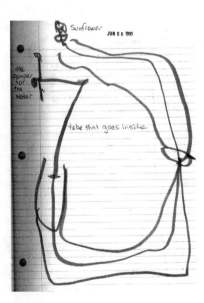

Figure 3.9.   Example of a journal entry.

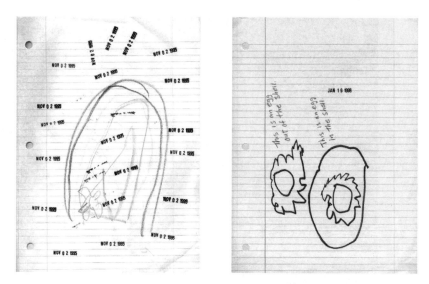

Figure 3.10. Date stamps used to decorate (left) and as science tools (right).

Journals are great tools for recording observations and predictions; however, there are things to consider before you start using them. First, journals do not need to be introduced at the very beginning of the school year. Each class is different, and you are the best judge of whether your students are ready to try to record their observations in this way. Also, if journaling does not go well at a particular point or with a particular activity, wait and try again with another activity. Journals are an important part of a PrePS classroom, but children need not record everything they do in this manner. Other types of recording can be used instead of, or in conjunction with, journals. The class can work together to make graphs, charts, and models. In the activity described in Activity 3.1, children's observations about an apple could be paired with photos of the outside of the apple. The class's predictions can be written alongside photos of the inside of the apple. These lists seem to foster a feeling of accomplishment; children often ask teachers and parents to "read me what I predicted" from the charts.

Even very young children can participate in recording activities. In one classroom, a teacher of 2- and 3-year-old children guided her students through observations and predictions about the insides of strawberries, apples, and carrots. Their observations of the outsides of these items were charted next to photographs of the objects. The chart also included predictions about the insides of the objects and the observations of the insides (see Figure 3.11). Although maintaining a journal is not reasonable for this young age group, some 3-year-old children can record observations of simple objects by drawing (see Figure 3.8), and all can participate in the creation of class lists and charts.

PLANNING FOR THE SCIENCE PRACTICES

There are some tools teachers can use to support their efforts to incorporate more science into their classrooms. The curriculum web discussed in Chapter 2 is an ex-

Date: April 18, 2001

	Observe outside	Predict inside	Check inside	
	Seeds are outside Red Green leaves on top	Different than yellow inside A little bit dark yellow	White Red Hole in the middle	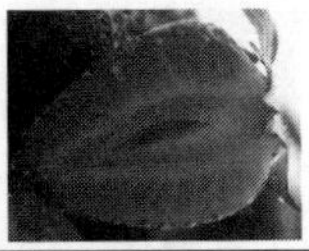
	Red skin "O" shaped 1 stem on top Skin has dots	Big inside Red inside 3 seeds inside It will look like a carrot	Looks like a butterfly White inside Hole for seeds 8 seeds	
	Orange skin Flowers grow on top Looks like a stick	It will have a truck inside It will look cracked inside	A little green inside Mostly orange	

Figure 3.11.   An observe-predict-check chart created with 2- and 3-year-olds.

ample. Another is the science practices planning grid (see Figure 3.12). The grid is a guide for designing learning experiences that support multiple science practices. When we plan activities, we use the grid to remind us to think about ways that particular content can be explored using different modes of talking and working. Sometimes an activity does not clearly support one of the science practices, which is fine. If there is a blank in the grid, however, the teacher could spend a little time pondering whether there is a way to fill it by extending activities to meet more learning goals.

By using the grid repeatedly, across different content throughout the year, teachers ensure that children have many opportunities to use the science practices. Remember, content and practice go together. By exploring similar content through different practices and using the same practices to explore different content, children learn both more thoroughly and more deeply. This understanding will serve them well as they move on to new content and explorations in school and throughout their lives.

Activities 3.3 and 3.4 provide specific instructions for some successful PrePS experiences. We developed these grids when we introduced PrePS into new school sites. Although one hallmark of PrePS that we have described elsewhere (Gelman & Brenneman, 2004) is that it is not prescriptive, we have found that newcomers to the program appreciate specific, extended examples of what we mean when we say "conceptually connected learning experiences that allow children to engage in authentic science practices over time." Although the activities may look lengthy and involved, please note that they include some repetition of information between the summaries, procedures, and grid itself. Also, some activities present multiple, related learning experiences that take place over a few days or longer. As you plan for your class, you will probably only need to use the grid itself (see Figure 3.12) to specify the ways that your learning experience supports particular science practices.

SCIENCE PRACTICES PLANNING GRID

SCIENCE PRACTICE 🌱	Concept/focus: Experience:
OBSERVE, PREDICT, CHECK 🔍	
COMPARE, CONTRAST, EXPERIMENT 🌸	
VOCABULARY, DISCOURSE, LANGUAGE 💬	
COUNTING, MEASUREMENT, AND MATH 📏	
RECORDING AND DOCUMENTING 📓	

Figure 3.12. Science practices planning grid.

Note: As always, these materials are meant as illustrations. If you like them, use them as they are, or use them as a jumping-off point for your own ideas and planning. If you would rather plan your own activities, use the blank grid provided in Figure 3.12. You can also adapt it to make it a better tool for you to design powerful learning experiences for your students.

Introducing Observation

This activity guide was developed using actual transcripts from a number of teachers' lessons. Our idea is to describe the essence of this introductory activity, rather than provide a true script. As always, we hope that our materials will provide a framework that you can adapt to your own needs.

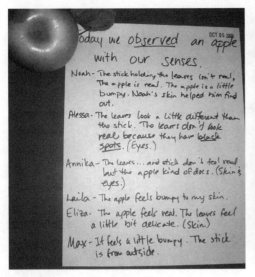
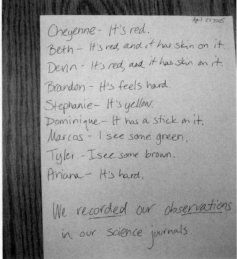

Figure 3.1A. Apple observation chart.

PROCEDURE

Begin the activity by showing an apple and telling the class that everyone is going to observe it. After introducing the word *observe*, ask the children if they know what it means. Likely, they will not, but take suggestions and then tell the children what it actually means (i.e., notice, use senses to find out about an object). You might need to spend some time talking about senses. Allow the children to tell you about the senses as much as possible and go over the function of each sense.

MATERIALS

- An apple or enough apples for each child to have one

- Paper or poster board for an observation chart

- Notebooks for each child, if introducing journals

- A date stamp, if introducing journals

- Let the children know that you are going to write down or record their observations on a chart. At the top of chart write something such as, "We *observed* an apple." Date the chart and tell children that you are writing the date so that later they will know on which day they observed the apple and the different observations that they made.

- Pass the apple around the group (or give each child an apple) and ask each child, "What do you notice about the apple?" or "What is your observation about the apple?" If answers begin to get repetitive, ask children to try to think of something else but do not push this too much. Record each child's name and his or her observation. Use prompts if necessary: What color is the apple? How does it feel? Is it smooth or rough? Hot or cold? Does it feel heavy to you? If a child does not want to make an observation, that is fine. As they watch and listen to peers, children become much more comfortable speaking up. You could also try asking these children to discuss the apple individually with you at a later time.

- When the children have all made observations, reintroduce the idea of recording (i.e., "writing down") and review the observations the children made (see Figure A3.1).

- Finally, set the stage for the next activity: "Tomorrow we are going to think about what is inside the apple."

You can also use this activity to introduce children to science journals. If you would like the children to make a record of their initial science activities, see pp. 48–50 for ways to do this.

SCIENCE PRACTICES PLANNING GRID: Activity 3.1

SCIENCE PRACTICE	*Concept/focus:* Introductory activities set the stage for later PrePS experiences *Experience:* Observing an apple
OBSERVE, PREDICT, CHECK	This simple activity is used to introduce children to the words *observe* and *observation* and to observation as a science practice. The teacher encourages children to use different senses by thinking about all aspects the apple's features: What color is the apple? How does it feel? Is it smooth or rough? Hot or cold? Does it feel heavy to you? and so forth.
COMPARE, CONTRAST, EXPERIMENT	This science practice is not the main focus of this activity.
VOCABULARY, DISCOURSE, LANGUAGE	After introducing the word *observe,* ask the children if they know what it means. Likely, they don't, but take suggestions and then tell what it actually means (e.g., notice, use our senses to find out about an object). Vary your way of asking—"What do you observe about the apple?" "What do you notice about the apple?" "What can you tell me about the apple?" "What is your observation?"—so that children develop a broader understanding of what it means to make observations. Introduce and encourage varied vocabulary to describe the apple.
COUNTING, MEASUREMENT, AND MATH	This science practice is not the main focus of this activity.
RECORDING AND DOCUMENTING	The teacher records the children's observations on a chart, which can serve as the beginning of an "observe, predict, check" chart when children cut the apple open in a later activity (see Activity 3.2). Children are introduced to the idea that scientists date their work when the teacher dates the observation chart. We tell children that we are writing the date so that later we will know which day we observed the apple and the different observations that we made. Children also use a date stamp to date their science journal entries. The teacher can transcribe what children say about their drawings. If you are with them while they draw, you can gently guide their efforts by asking them to think about what color crayon they will need to record this apple, to describe the shape of the apple, and to describe its parts. Use the observation chart, too, if children aren't sure what to record: "Let's see what we observed about the apple. We can read our chart. Maybe that will help you decide what to draw."

Making Predictions

This activity continues children's introduction to observing, predicting, and checking using apples (see Activity 3.1).

PROCEDURE

Start the activity by reviewing what *observe* means and the observations made the day before (see Activity 3.1). Review children's observations about the apple by reading the observation chart. Doing this also illustrates a function of print; it helps them know what they did the day before.

Teachers introduce the idea of *prediction*. Tell children that they will be predicting what is inside the apple,

MATERIALS

- A few apples of the same type used for the previous observation activity

- A knife and cutting board

- Poster board or paper for prediction chart

and ask if they know what *predict* means. Explain that it is kind of like a guess: When we predict, we do not know the answer or what is definitely going to happen, but we usually have some information that helps to make a prediction. Because they have observed the outside of the apple and because they have seen inside apples in the past, they can guess (predict) what the apple might look and feel like underneath the peel.

Explain that when they use their senses to notice what color the outside of the apple is, that is an *observation*, but when they guess the color that the inside will be, that is a *prediction*. Teachers should try to make the point that predictions do not have to be right, but they should be sensible.

As children make predictions, the teacher can record these on a chart (see Figure A3.2). If need be, the teacher should elicit a variety of predictions by asking questions such as, "What will it look like under the red part? What will it smell like? How do you think the apple will feel to your skin?"

Once predictions are completed, ask children what they should do to check their predictions and to find out for sure what is inside this apple. Although the teacher could easily just cut the apple, asking children this question allows them to think about a simple problem and share their ideas for solving it.

Once the idea of cutting with a knife is mentioned, cut the apple open. When the apple is cut open, children check their predictions by observing the inside of the apple. Use the prediction chart to guide the observations. "Jamir predicted the apple would be juicy inside. Do you see juice inside, Jamir? Does the apple feel juicy and wet?" "Natasha thought that a worm might live inside the apple. That was a great prediction. Natasha, is there a worm in this apple?"

After completing the observe-predict-check sequence, the activity can be extended in a number of ways. Children can use jour-

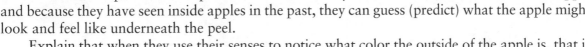

Figure A3.2 Apple prediction chart.

nals to record their observations of the inside of the apple. Teachers can also ask children to make predictions about how the apple will taste, whether it will be crunchy or soft, and so forth. At snack time, let them eat the apples to check their predictions (see also Activity 4.1).

SCIENCE PRACTICES PLANNING GRID: Activity 3.2

SCIENCE PRACTICE	*Concept/focus:* Introductory activities set the stage for later PrePS experiences. *Experience:* Inside an apple
OBSERVE, PREDICT, CHECK	Children review observations from a previous lesson in which they observed the outside of an apple. Make a new chart for predictions and observations of the inside of the apple. Children are introduced to the idea of prediction as a special kind of guess, and they predict what is on the inside of an apple. Children are asked how we can check the predictions, then the apple is cut open. Children use their observational skills to check their predictions.
COMPARE, CONTRAST, EXPERIMENT	These science practices are not the main focus of the activity, but they could be highlighted in an extension in which children compare and contrast the outsides, insides, and tastes of different apple varieties.
VOCABULARY, DISCOURSE, LANGUAGE	Children will be introduced to the ideas and terms "predict" and "prediction." Future activities will reinforce the meanings of the words and practice using the procedures. Encourage children to make a variety of observations and predictions, and to use varied vocabulary, by asking questions that focus attention on a variety of features, e.g., "What will it look like under the red part? Do you think you will smell anything? Will it feel wet or dry when you touch it?"
COUNTING, MEASUREMENT, AND MATH	Children can predict the numbers of seeds in each apple and check their predictions by counting. Teachers might want to write these numbers down, then ask children to compare across the apples. Do they all have the same number of seeds? Which apple had the fewest seeds? What is the largest number of seeds that the children found? How many seeds did we find altogether?
RECORDING AND DOCUMENTING	Emphasize that, like scientists, we record things to keep track of our ideas, show our parents, and look at them later to remind us of the ideas we had. Date charts and journals and take the opportunity to review why it's important to date our work. Children can observe and draw the inside of the apple in their science journals.

61

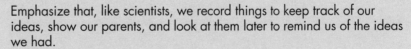

Preschool Pathways to Science (PrePS™): Facilitating Scientific Ways of Thinking, Talking, Doing, and Understanding by Rochel Gelman, Kimberly Brenneman, Gay Macdonald, and Moisés Román. Copyright © 2010 Paul H. Brookes Publishing Co., Inc. All rights reserved.

The Blubber Glove Experiment

This activity allows children to explore the insulation properties of blubber and other materials and to carry out a simple experiment.

PROCEDURE

To set the stage for this activity, teachers discuss how people and animals stay warm in the winter. This can happen during an earlier group time.

During group time, briefly review what you have discussed about animals keeping warm. Then introduce the concept of blubber and let children know that you will be doing an investigation to find out more about blubber.

The experiment involves filling double-layered, sealed plastic bags with solid vegetable shortening ("blubber"). Children will be able to slide one hand into a glove with blubber and one into a glove without blubber. Then they place their hands into a bucket or cooler of icy water.

Before doing the experiment, have children predict whether blubber or no blubber will keep their hands warmer.

MATERIALS

- Plastic bags with press-and-seal closures
- Duct tape (optional)
- Large can of vegetable shortening
- Feathers or other insulating material (preferably nonwhite color for contrast with blubber [optional])
- Large bucket, cooler, or sensory table
- Bag of ice
- Poster board for creating results chart
- Paper towels
- Digital camera to record procedure (optional)

- Create the blubber gloves by lining the sides of a bag with shortening. Be sure that the insulating material thoroughly covers the sides. Turn a second bag inside out, insert it inside the first, and zip the two together. Taping the top of the bags with duct tape will help ensure that accidental openings do not occur. Make a second glove with two bags but no filling.

- Place ice and some water into the bucket, cooler, or sensory table. Have children wear one type of glove on their left hand and one on the right and insert their hands into water. (You might want to hold children's hands lightly to keep them from submersing them under the water line.) Ask them to tell you when one hand is getting cold. Which hand is it? Which glove keeps their hands warmer? Record their findings on a chart (see Figure 3.3).

Teachers can extend the learning and the opportunity to practice experimental procedures by varying the substances in the gloves (feathers versus no feathers or blubber versus feathers). These new experiments should take place over a number of days using different glove combinations.

SCIENCE PRACTICES PLANNING GRID: Activity 3.3

SCIENCE PRACTICE	*Concept/focus:* Seasonal change/animal adaptations *Experience:* Blubber gloves
OBSERVE, PREDICT, CHECK	After discussing ways that people and animals stay warm in winter or in cold environments (e.g., blubber, feathers, fur) over a few days, introduce the blubber gloves and tell children they are going to do an experiment to find out more about blubber. Describe the test procedure. Ask children to predict which glove will keep their hands warmer.
COMPARE, CONTRAST, EXPERIMENT	Ask children to describe how their hands feel in the water. Is one of their hands getting cold? Which one? Which glove keeps their hands warm? The experiment can be repeated on another day using feathers versus no feathers, feathers versus blubber, and so forth. Eventually, you can assess children's understanding of the basic experimental procedure by giving them materials (two kinds of gloves and a cooler filled with ice water) and asking them to find out which kind works better to keep their hands warm. In other words, the children design their own test, and the teacher assesses whether they choose to use two different gloves simultaneously.
VOCABULARY, DISCOURSE, LANGUAGE	Practice descriptive language, including *warm* and *cold*. *Blubber* is likely to be a new word for them.
COUNTING, MEASUREMENT, AND MATH	When children review the results charts (described in next section), they can compare the results for each kind of glove by counting. For blubber versus no blubber, this will likely be zero (for the no-blubber glove) versus another number (for the blubber glove) because the shortening is a far better insulator than the bags alone. However, if the test is done with blubber and feathers, for example, the numbers will be closer and more challenging to compare.
RECORDING AND DOCUMENTING	Make a results chart for each experiment. Teachers can write the question, "Which gloves keep our hands warmer?" Then they can create a column for each kind of glove (e.g., blubber, no blubber) used in the test and use words and/or photos to label columns. Children can write their names under the word or photo that corresponds to their finding. The charts can be used to review findings later. Involve children as much as possible by asking them to tell what they found, then link that to the chart (e.g., "Oh, yes, here's your name under the picture of the blubber glove. Sasha found out the blubber glove kept her hand warmer"). Taking pictures during the experiments allows teachers to show pictures later to assess retention of key ideas. Asking children to describe what they were doing, what they were trying to find out, and what they found provides information about each child's understanding of a simple experimental procedure.

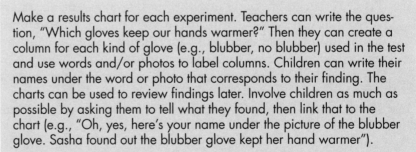

Animate/Inanimate Distinction Activity Using Wind-Up Toys

These activities encourage children to think and talk about the many differences between animate and inanimate objects. The story, *Alexander and the Wind-Up Mouse,* by Leo Lionni, provides many opportunities to compare and contrast the appearance, behaviors, and capabilities of a real animal with those of a wind-up toy replica. It also supports learning of new words and concepts (e.g., *key*—often called the winding thing or something similar by children) and discussions of emotions (e.g., *envy, having a heavy heart*). Extension activities allow children to predict what they believe is inside a toy mouse and to check their predictions.

PROCEDURE

Before you read the story to the children, take time to identify points in the story to stop and ask questions about; for example, whether toys need to eat, whether they can move by themselves, whether they need to sleep. Read the book interactively with children, by asking questions about the characters and new words, as described earlier.

   As an extension activity, ask children to think about and describe what is inside a real mouse and what is inside a wind-up mouse.

Figure A3.4 Journal entries incorporate a new shape and a new word to describe it.

MATERIALS

- Copy of *Alexander and the Wind-Up Mouse* by Leo Lionni

- Wind-up toy(s)

- Small hammer

- Strong plastic bags with press-and-seal closures (freezer bags work well)

- Magnifying glasses

They are likely to be quite good at this, knowing that blood, bones, and food are inside a real mouse and gears, batteries, and wires might be inside a wind-up mouse. Encourage children to think about ways to find out for sure what is inside a wind-up toy. Then open one up. We have had success with the following procedure: Place a toy inside the freezer bag and seal it, for safety reasons. Use the hammer to crack the case of the toy. The bag will catch small pieces that might break off. Remove the toy and finish opening it with your hands. Children enjoy exploring the gears and mechanisms they find inside the toy. Encourage children to use magnifying glasses to identify and describe what they find inside. This provides a great illustration of the way that this science tool helps us observe details.

65

SCIENCE PRACTICES PLANNING GRID: Activity 3.4

SCIENCE PRACTICE	Concept/focus: Animate-inanimate distinction	
	Experience: Alexander & the Wind-Up Mouse by Leo Lionni	Experience: Wind-up toys
OBSERVE, PREDICT, CHECK	During circle time, children observe and describe pictures of Alexander and Willy. Create chart of observations.	Predict what is on the inside of a wind-up toy. Ask how children can check. Open toys in small groups.
COMPARE, CONTRAST, EXPERIMENT	Ask planned questions that lead children to compare and contrast key characteristics of animate (Alexander) and inanimate (Willy) objects.	Discuss differences between real and wind-up animals (e.g., looks, abilities, movement).
DISCOURSE, VOCABULARY, LANGUAGE	Define and discuss terms from story (e.g., *key, envy, heavy heart*). Emphasize comparisons and contrasts to encourage use of comparative language (e.g., *soft/hard, real/pretend*).	Model and encourage use of comparative language. New word (*spiral*) is introduced.
COUNTING, MEASUREMENT, AND MATH		
RECORDING AND DOCUMENTING	Review the observation chart created previously. Journal entries	Use journals to record the insides of wind-up toys. Encourage children who are ready to practice writing skills to label their recordings.

4

Getting Started
and Moving Forward

When we began introducing Preschool Pathways to Science (PrePS™) to teachers, we encountered practical issues that required us to rethink and expand our approach. PrePS was originally developed as a framework to help teachers design their own stand alone comprehensive and novel curriculum, but a number of teachers told us that they could not do this. Some were overwhelmed by the idea of designing their own curriculum. Others worked in schools that already had a comprehensive curriculum; they were interested in using PrePS to enhance, not replace, that curriculum.

In essence, our response to the two issues is the same. We know that choosing central concepts, focuses, and learning experiences that connect together in a meaningful way is one of the more challenging parts of PrePS. It often requires a shift in thinking about themes to thinking about science concepts, and this can take some adjustment. Our advice is to start by integrating the science practices into your classroom activities. Begin observing, predicting, investigating, experimenting, and recording. You will become more comfortable supporting children's thinking, talking, and working in scientific ways. As this becomes easier, and as you see how students are responding positively, you can move into choosing a central concept and planning conceptually connected learning activities around it. For teachers who use another comprehensive curriculum, we similarly suggest incorporating the science practices into ongoing activities. Help children look for and find connections between and among ideas and activities. This change in approach, by itself, will benefit young learners.

When we take PrePS to new schools we find that teachers quite readily pick up and use certain aspects of the program. Among the science practices, teachers seem especially enthusiastic about incorporating journals and documenting, likely because these are also good literacy practices. Many teachers are already prepared to support language and literacy growth because these are emphasized in teacher preparation and professional development courses. Journals and documenting seem familiar because they map onto, and extend, what teachers already know and do.

GETTING STARTED WITH PrePS

To repeat, PrePS is not a prescribed curriculum. Instead, it supports the creativity and uniqueness of children and individual teachers. It also respects teachers' knowledge of their students and ways to teach them. We realize, however, that we need to provide structure for educators who are just being introduced to PrePS. The best way to illustrate our conceptual approach in a way that supports understanding is to provide multiple, redundant examples—just as we suggest teachers do for their students. This chapter presents a lot of examples. These illustrate PrePS in action and address some common questions: How do I start PrePS in my classroom? How do I continue? What are some examples of long-term plans?

Materials and Tools

Our approach to science in preschool is that it is related to our everyday lives—a philosophy that is reflected in the materials we use for our activities. Starting to use PrePS involves having certain tools and materials accessible for children's use, but these need not be expensive. Most of what you will use can be found at the grocery or discount store. Some of the observation and measuring tools may already be in your classroom, which will come in handy as you introduce using tools with purpose. Although PrePS does not require fancy science equipment, some simple tools can enhance a wide variety of science experiences. Magnifying glasses and tabletop magnifiers will be useful for investigations of small objects and allow students to see patterns, textures, and tiny parts more easily. Simple measurement tools (e.g., pan balances, rulers, measuring cups and spoons) are often incorporated into PrePS experiences.

One tool you definitely will want to have is a science journal for each child. Use the type of notebook you prefer (e.g., blank pages, lines for writing). A supply of crayons and colored pencils also should be available. It may be difficult to keep these in good working order or to pay for multiple sets, but they really improve the quality of children's journal entries. With them, children can find the right color to represent what they are observing without having to wait too long.

A science-oriented classroom has measurement and observation tools throughout the room and playground, not only at the science table or in a discovery area. Just as creativity occurs in places other than the dramatic play and art areas, opportunities to think and work mathematically and scientifically occur beyond the science table. Children should have access to their journals when they want to record something about their science observations or learning.

As described in Chapter 3, tools that invite observation and measurement should be added throughout your classroom. The intended use of science tools is unlikely to be discovered without some guidance from the teacher—although the children may figure out creative ways to use them anyway (see Figure 4.1). Provide information about their functions by incorporating tools into science activities. You can also informally reinforce their functions when children use them at the sensory table, in their dramatic play, in the block area, and in other areas of the room and play yard. If you add measuring cups to the sandbox, for example, spend some time working with children so that they know what is special about these particular scoops. Children will not always use these tools to measure, but they should know that measur-

Figure 4.1. *Measuring cups aren't always used to measure.*

ing is possible. You can revisit this idea during cooking activities. By providing guidance along with the tools, a teacher encourages children to become familiar with science and math tools, to explore the jobs they do, and to consider everyday activities in scientific and mathematical ways. To illustrate what can happen, children from a PrePS classroom were observed during an outdoor play session spontaneously using a variety of tools to explore the objects and events around them. Some were using magnifying glasses to inspect piles of leaves, looking to see if any creatures lived in them. Another group was digging, using rulers to measure the length of the worms they found and observing the worms' bodies with magnifiers.

Some tools are easier to introduce than others. The function of magnifying glasses and table magnifiers is relatively straightforward. Children will have some fun just making things look bigger. Although they may not limit the magnifiers' use to very small objects and details, children will still get the general idea of how to use the tool and how to interpret their findings. Measurement tools are more difficult in this regard. Their proper use and interpretation is not obvious. Take time to consider how to talk about these tools accurately, but simply, and be sure to provide multiple guided opportunities to incorporate the tools into science explorations. If possible, introduce tools by linking them to something children already know. Recall from Chapter 3 that magnifiers can be introduced as a way to extend one's visual experience, and balance scales can be introduced as a way to observe and compare the heaviness of objects. As another example, if your science explorations lead you to want to use thermometers, think about how you could introduce this tool so

Box 4.1
INTRODUCING THE THERMOMETER

If you decide to use a thermometer as part of science explorations, one way to introduce it is to have children feel two cups of water—one cold and one warm. After they identify the difference between the two, insert a thermometer in each cup. (Be sure the thermometers can safely register the temperature of the warm water.) Have children observe the difference between the two thermometers.

Children already know that the water cups have different temperatures, so they can link the difference in the "red lines" to that knowledge. A bigger (or taller, higher, larger) line means *hotter.* A smaller (or shorter, lower) line means *colder.* Have children play with this new idea by predicting what will happen to the thermometer in the cool water if you move it to the warm water. Predict whether a thermometer in the sun will have a bigger red line than one in the shade. Find out.

You do not need to introduce the numbers on the thermometer, but children might be interested in them. If so, try to link these numbers to their prior understandings (e.g., "Is it a cold day outside? What number does the thermometer say? 20? Yes, 20 degrees is very cold. On a warm day the temperature is much higher. The number of degrees will be a much larger number"). If you do talk about the numbers, point out that when it is warm, the red line on the thermometer goes higher and gets longer. As children have more experience using thermometers to measure their own observations of hot and cold temperatures, the numbers are more likely to become meaningful to them. Note that preschool children will not develop full understandings, but relevant experience can serve them well as they move ahead in school.

it is tied to children's own observations about the world (see Box 4.1). The key point is the same as for all good teaching: Build on previous lessons and extend them; present information that can be bridged to existing knowledge.

Planning Connected Learning Experiences

The most important thing you need to start PrePS is a plan for where you are going. Whether you design a full curriculum using webs and weekly planning sheets (see Figure 2.4) or start by incorporating science practices into your ongoing activities, you will need to think about the conceptual connections you hope children will make and the experiences you can provide to meet your learning goals for your students. The brainstorming required is often enhanced when colleagues work together to define learning goals and to generate ways to support children's learning. Collaboration among colleagues, although not critical to the success of PrePS, does make success more likely. Regular meetings provide opportunities to do this.

Support is also helpful if you run into a roadblock. A fresh perspective on a problem can mean the difference between working through to a solution or giving up. Investment in a new program by many people improves success rates and increases the chances that the program will be perpetuated. However, if your colleagues do not want to work with PrePS, you still can do so. Under these circumstances, you might want to start with the science practices and familiar content, then move to planning a concept web when you are more comfortable with the approach.

Not surprisingly, PrePS classrooms can look very different depending on the teacher and children involved. The conceptual content being explored will vary, of course, but the experience level of the participants also has a great effect. A teacher who is new to PrePS will implement it differently than one who has been using it for years and who is comfortable with it. The age group you work with will also affect the learning goals you have and the experiences you provide to meet these goals. For these reasons, we cannot anticipate the exact situation in your classroom, but we hope to provide enough information so that you can adapt the PrePS approach to your specific circumstances.

EARLY PrePS LEARNING EXPERIENCES

Regardless of the particular circumstances, we often try to begin PrePS similarly at the beginning of the school year. As described in Chapter 3, when we start PrePS with a new group of students, we introduce *observation* and *observe* (see Activity 3.1). Next, we introduce the terms *prediction* and *predict* (see Activity 3.2). Both of these experiences incorporate other science practices, most notably documentation as teachers write down children's observations and predictions. We often introduce journals at this point, too. Apples are relatively simple items for children to try to draw, which makes them a good topic for early entries (see Figure 4.2).

Figure 4.2. Very early journal entries.

Introducing Observation, Prediction, and Documentation

These early experiences are really foundational because observing, predicting, and documenting will continue to be practiced throughout children's PrePS experiences, into elementary science, and beyond. For this reason, we do not rush these introductory activities. They might take a few days, or they could take much longer. There is no set pace. As always, you respond to your own class's needs and interests.

After the introductory PrePS activities (Activity 4.1 builds on Activities 3.1 and 3.2), your class's explorations can go in many different directions. Connect the content of these new experiences to what came before, and incorporate the science practices as much as possible. If you have chosen a central concept to explore across many months, then you will want to choose a focus that links to the early observation and prediction activities and that will connect to other focuses that you plan to explore.

Where Do We Go from Here?

In this section, we provide extended examples of explorations that can follow the introductory PrePS experiences. Each set of learning experiences was developed and implemented under very different circumstances; taken together, they illustrate the flexibility of our approach. Teachers in a wide range of situations can use PrePS to support children's learning, and they can adapt the content of the experiences to the needs and interests of their students.

In Box 4.2, the first set of learning activities continues the exploration of insides and outsides using a wide range of materials and provides practice using the observe-predict-check sequence. A second example similarly concentrates on insides and outsides, but the conceptual focuses are explored in a more extended, in-depth manner. The third set of experiences continues an investigation of apples, which connects to pears and pumpkins as part of a larger autumn theme, when some aspects of PrePS were applied to an existing theme-based curriculum. In the final example, the central concept is form and function, with a focus on senses as tools for investigating and making observations about the world.

The example in Box 4.2 is from one of our earliest introductions of PrePS in a new school site. To illustrate the PrePS approach, we came to the school twice a week and engaged the children in large-group discussions, then extended these experiences with small-group activities. We also talked with teachers about ways to continue working with the science ideas and procedures throughout the week. This school already used a comprehensive curriculum, so our efforts were to enrich that curriculum with meaningful, connected science learning experiences.

Box 4.2 presents our notes on the goals of the activities, the reactions of the children and teachers, and the science practices in which we engaged. The activity series (exploring the insides and outsides of a variety of objects in the world) provided a natural way to practice observing, predicting, and checking. As covered already, we know that children can go beyond surface features to categorize objects, if they know about them. These activities allowed us to build more specific knowledge about the internal, non-surface characteristics of different kinds of things. They also provided practice thinking about the ways that certain kinds of surface features do and do not predict internal characteristics.

From this activity, you could go in a number of directions. For example, you could move into explorations of the ways these things grow and change, or how living things are different from nonliving things. Exploring the insides and outsides of machines allows children to take apart things like typewriters, telephones, and wind-up toys to explore how they work. These hands-on explorations may lead into discussions of what is inside different kinds of things that allows them to work and move. The key to maximizing learning is to keep experiences connected conceptually and by the science practices.

Related Focuses

Another teaching team connected a focus on apples with one on nuts and another on human beings. The various focuses were connected by opportunities to engage in science practices and to discuss the differences between the insides and outsides of particular objects. Exploring a different kind of object (other than an apple) provided

Box 4.2
PRACTICING OBSERVATION AND PREDICTION BY EXPLORING INSIDES AND OUTSIDES

- **March 5:** Introduce *observe* and *observation*. Discuss using senses to make observations. Each child makes an observation about the apple. These are recorded on a chart. Introduce journals in small groups. Ask children to journal their observations of the apple.

- **March 7:** Introduce *predict* and *check*. Children predict what is inside the apple. Predictions are recorded (including number of seeds when children predict seeds). Cut open the apple to check. Record children's observations of the inside of the apple. Discuss links between predictions and observations. Journal the findings in small groups.

  Notes: The children engaged in a fabulous spontaneous discussion about the possible consequences of eating seeds. One says that if you eat an apple seed a tree will not grow inside of you. When probed, the child's reasoning is that it could happen "only if we give ourselves some water and dirt."

- **March 14:** Observe the outside of a tomato. Record observations. Predict what is inside the tomato. Record predictions. Cut open the tomato to check predictions. Record observations. Journal both the outside and the inside of the tomato.

  Notes: The assistant teacher decided to make paper tomato plants for the children. One student used these as props in dramatic play. He acted out growing and having his fruit picked!

- **March 19:** Start the inside and outside fruit chart to further solidify the observe-predict-check cycle. Use apple, kiwi, lime, plum, and strawberry. Focus observations on color and whether seeds are visible and, if so, how many. On the first day children make these observations about the outside of each fruit, then predict what is inside. These are written down and the children glue them to the chart. Children journal the fruit(s) of their choice.

- **March 20:** Cut open fruit to check predictions. Chart the observations. Introduce books as a way to check information if you can't do it yourself (e.g., you couldn't check the insides of an animal, but you could find a book that would show you). Use a book that is about the characteristics of different fruits (e.g., *Fruit* [De Bourgoing, 1991]; see Box 3.7, p. 47). Show the front cover and have children predict what the book is about by observing the outside. Children journal the inside of fruit of their choice. Ask the teacher to look through the book with children throughout the week (e.g., during group time).

- **March 25:** During the previous weeks, children had enjoyed using their ears to "hear" fruit. When a teacher mentioned that one could actually hear a coconut, children requested that they have the chance to explore one. So we will make observations about the outside of the coconut. We will give each child a picture that represents one sense (e.g., eye, ear, nose, skin) and ask the child to observe the coconut using only that sense. These observations are recorded. Predictions about the inside of the coconut are made. What does the "juice" inside look like, and so forth? The coconut

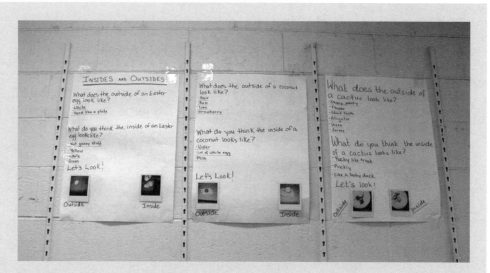

Figure 4.3. Observation charts about insides and outsides.

is cracked open, and the inside is observed. A few volunteers taste the coconut. Their observations are recorded (see Figure 4.3). Journal entries are completed (see Activity 4.2).

Notes: Having noted that the teacher in the room for younger children is doing a lot of science activities with the children, we photograph the walls there. Children are observing the inside and outside of bird eggs. They predict what will happen to the egg. Also, they are growing an amaryllis, keeping track of its height. When doing this activity in the younger classroom, the teacher used the whole coconut for observation and prediction. The inside was observed, and she charted everything. Later she tells us that one student informed her that he had learned (from watching a cooking show on television) that the "juice" is called coconut water—it is only milk if you squeeze the white part.

- **March 26:** We have learned a lot about seeds and fruit. We know that usually the seeds are inside of the fruit, but we wonder what is inside of a seed? Observe, predict, and check sunflower and pumpkin seeds. Make journal entries about the seeds.

Notes: The teacher would like to have her students sort seeds and then incorporate them into art projects. Also, the teacher will read the book we found about pumpkin life cycles later in the week. The teacher in the younger classroom asked her students to observe the outside of an Easter egg and to make predictions about the inside of the egg. She made a poster that recorded the children's observations and includes photos.

- **April 2:** We talk with children about the idea that we can observe other people and predict what someone is feeling inside from his or her expression on the outside. Have the adult make faces first, and children observe, predict, and check. Then children try to convey an emotion through their face and posture. Different faces are drawn in the journals.

- **April 4:** We review our conversation about using faces and body posture to predict how another person is feeling. Then we move on to talk some more about seeds. Read about seeds and plant life cycles in *The Tiny Seed* by Eric Carle (2005; see Box 3.8, p. 46).

  Note: We asked children to journal and talk about the plant life cycle. This was basically to get a measure of their base rate of knowledge with plans to reassess as relevant activities are completed.

- **April 9:** Bring in garden plant and cactus with roots exposed. Have children observe the garden plant that grew from a seed, just like the flower in the book. Record observations. Start to segue into desert plants (e.g., "Why couldn't the seed in the book grow in the desert?").

  Notes: One student pointed out that cacti grow in the desert and another posited that cacti are not plants. It's like they read the lesson plan! We decide to explore this question by observing the cactus to determine whether it has the same parts as the garden plant. We make observations and these are recorded. Then we note that they both have roots. One student declares that the cactus has a stem—"it's just a very fat stem." We look at a book that confirms his idea and that tells us that the needles or spines of a cactus are really a type of leaf. Given that information, everyone agrees that cacti are plants. The children request that we cut open the cactus so we promise to do that tomorrow. We make predictions about what is inside the cactus. We journal the outside of the plants. This transcript is full of great discussion and is punctuated by a debate between students about whether the needles on a cactus are like the thorns on a thorn bush or the needles on a Christmas tree. Great stuff!

- **April 10:** Review predictions. Cut open the cactus. Record observations. Journal observations (see Figure 4.4).

  Note: Teacher tells us that a student's parents have asked that we be sure to take pictures of the inside of the cactus. They say she's been talking about it all night. Assistant teacher brings in some ocean items for the kids, including a horseshoe crab, a skate egg sac, and a whelk egg sac. One student suggests that we should "observate" what is inside the latter. This is a term he has used before. We do so and find tiny whelks in that egg sac. The skate sac is disappointing, however. The ocean is a topic of great interest to the children, many of whom spend summer days at the New Jersey shore.

- **April 16:** Review vocabulary and all of the items we have investigated. (Coincidentally, the children were discussing memories when we arrived.) We want to allow children to think about the outsides and insides of animals, too. Although we usually design PrePS activities that allow children to work and think about things in their immediate environment, the children show great interest in the desert so we build on our cactus explorations to discuss "an animal that lives in the desert." Use photos to observe the outside of a camel. Record observations. Discuss hump. Predict what is inside the camel's hump. Record predictions. Also, discuss how many humps camels can have. "Real" camels have one or two, but "camels in our imagination or in Dr. Seuss books" can have more. Talk about how we can check predictions about humps. One student said: "We can't cut it open! There would be blood all over the carpet!" And another chimed in, "—and food!" (These comments match their inside-the-hump pre-

Figure 4.4.   Journaling what we observed inside a cactus.

dictions.) We arrive at the idea of using books or the Internet to research our question. We journal observations of the outside of a camel.

- **April 17:** Review names for one- and two-hump camels. This wasn't in the original plan, but one student called the Bactrian a "train" camel, so we wanted to work on this word for a bit. We told the children that "a *B* has two humps, just like a *Bactrian* camel." Review predictions about hump. Look at Ruiz's *Animals on the Inside* (1995; see Box 3.7) to check our predictions. Observe the drawings of the inside of a camel. Discuss that the inside of the hump is fat, which is stored when camels eat and drink. When they go without food and water, the fat is used for energy, just like in our bodies.

  Notes: We compared photographs of camels with large humps and some without. Which camel hasn't eaten for a long time? One student bent over and said he has a hump, so we pull his shirt up to make a big hump while he eats, then lower it when he cannot eat, and so forth.

Two undergraduate field study students ask about the program, offer insightful comments, and show interest in working with us. Another had mentioned earlier that the kids love to have their predictions read to them throughout the week (during lunch especially). We stop in to visit the younger children to take pictures of their cactus chart. The teacher shows us a book they have made about planting carrot seeds, predicting days until germination. She had earlier asked for the *Fruit* (De Bourgoing, 1991) and *Vegetables in the Garden* (De Bourgoing, 1994; see Box 3.8) books and reported that the kids loved them. They also enjoyed a debate about where the seeds are in various items including grass and carrots. (Tough ones!) Their ideas are recorded in their class book.

more experience thinking about and using these ideas and skills. It also provided an opportunity to compare across categories to find similarities and differences among apples, nuts, and human beings. One bridge between these focuses involved the outside covering on each object. Because human skin and nutshells have a similar range of colors, teachers thought the two focuses would provide a way to explore outside coverings and to emphasize their similar functions despite color differences. Learning was enhanced by the opportunity to think about the insides and outsides of very different kinds of objects, to compare and contrast within and across categories, and to think deeply about some common features (e.g., the function of skin, peels, and shells across biological kinds).

At the end of their explorations, the teachers decided to represent children's observations in a Venn diagram (i.e., intersecting circles). They listed children's descriptions of the features of nutshells on one side and human skin on the other side of the diagram. The children used these lists to find similarities to be added to the shared space in the center (see Figure 4.5). This visual representation of features helped review and solidify children's understandings of the similarities between the two kinds of "outsides" and the unique features of each. Some teachers were not sure that this kind of representation would be understood by 3- and 4-year-old children. However, the experience was successful because teachers allowed children to explore both objects, make observations, and build on a familiar science practice (recording observations) to introduce this new kind of representation (see Figure 4.6).

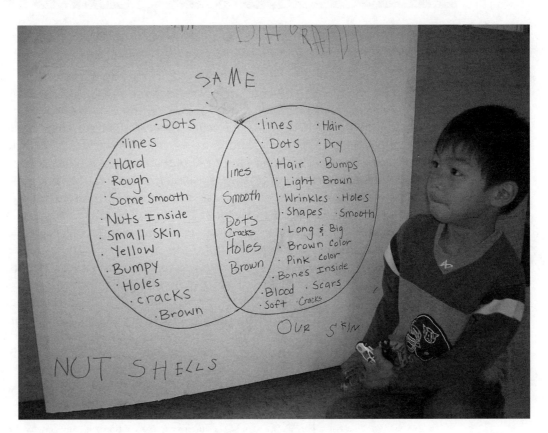

Figure 4.5. Comparing and contrasting nutshells and skin.

Figure 4.6.   Observing skin.

Nuts[1] were chosen as a focus for two other reasons. First, one of the teachers had explored them with students in another school and found that children were deeply interested in them. Second, the teachers wanted to launch an investigation that would allow them to introduce science tools to their students in a meaningful way. This investigation allowed children to use various science tools including magnifying glasses, measuring cups, tweezers, measuring tapes, and scales. They also used hammers, mallets, and nutcrackers to crack nuts open (see Figure 4.7), as well as mortars, pestles, and grinders to make nut butters. Note that these experiences using tools for various purposes would also fit nicely under the central concept of *form and function.* Because science concepts are richly interconnected, you will find these big ideas arising even when they are not the central concept you are exploring—providing more experiences for children to connect to new content.

The science practices of observing, predicting, and checking were clearly supported by this focus on nuts. Comparing and contrasting were well integrated; children spent a great deal of time discussing similarities and differences in the color, shape, texture, and size of the various nuts. Connections were made to the focus on human beings when children began to compare the colors of nuts to the colors of their own and their friends' skin. The Venn diagram showing shared and unique features of nutshells and human skin provided a visual representation of some of the

---

[1] No child in the class had an allergy to nuts. Be sure to exercise caution with any activity that involves tasting or handling food.

Figure 4.7. What's inside the nutshells?

similarities and differences between the two coverings. It also provided an introduction to a representational tool that children will encounter in their later school years. Mathematics skills were enhanced by opportunities to sort nuts along specific dimensions. Children also used tools to weigh and measure the length of nuts to make comparisons among types.

The science practice involving discourse, language, and vocabulary also was well supported by this series of explorations. As children observed and investigated the outsides and insides of nuts, they used many vocabulary words with meaning and in varied contexts. Some words were used to discuss and describe something about the nuts themselves: *shells, crack, roll, tree, size, large, small, big, little, shape, round, oval, texture, bumpy,* and *smooth;* other terms described processes: *measure, pour,* and *sort.* Children also were introduced to the names of tools and nuts: *mallet, grinder, almonds, cashews,* and *hazelnuts.* These vocabulary words were posted prominently so that parents could see them and use them with the children at home. It is not critical that children learn long lists of special names; however, when these words are part of ongoing explorations, children are likely to acquire them and use them appropriately. Evidence suggests that exposure to less commonly used words in the home is related to general vocabulary acquisition (Hart & Risley, 1995). This, in turn, is linked to reading achievement (Dickinson, 2001; Strickland & Riley-Ayers, 2006). The teachers in this classroom also incorporated a number of books into their explorations of nuts (see Box 4.3).

Related Thematic Content

Many teachers already use a comprehensive theme-based curriculum. For teachers who implement an autumn theme early in the school year, an exploration of apples is popular and can be extended to include other objects associated with autumn, such as pumpkins. Exploration of these items can be enhanced by giving children the opportunity to practice using the observe-predict-check sequence. Other science practices also can be woven into classroom activities. Box 4.4 presents highlights from a collection of learning experiences that were designed and implemented by one of our partner teachers who was integrating the PrePS approach with her school's curriculum for the first time.[2] They illustrate how PrePS strengthens the thematic exploration by incorporating key science practices, including those associated with higher-order thinking, mathematics, and literacy. These activities are noteworthy for a number of reasons. First, they are from the first PrePS classroom led by someone completely new to the program (who was not stepping into a school that already used PrePS). Although the research team provided support, this teacher was most definitely in charge and the researchers very rarely led learning activities. In addition,

---

Box 4.3
SOME BOOKS TO USE WHEN STUDYING NUTS

Aardema, V., & Cepeda, J. (2002). *Koi and the kola nuts.* New York: Simon & Schuster Children's Publishing.

Burns, D.L., & McGee, J.F. (1996). *Berries, nuts, and seeds.* Minnetonka, MN: NorthWood Press.

Coats, L.J. (1991). *The almond orchard.* New York: Simon & Schuster Children's Publishing.

Earle, O.L. (1975). *Nuts.* New York: Morrow.

Ehlert, L. (2004). *Nuts to you.* New York: Harcourt.

Poole, G.J. (1974). *Nuts from the forest, orchard, and field.* New York: Dodd, Mead.

White, K., & Cabban, V. (2004). *The nutty nut chase.* Intercourse, PA: Good Books.

---

[2]At the time she worked with us, Ines Louro taught at the Livingston Avenue Child Development Center in New Brunswick, New Jersey. She is now a speech correctionist with the Perth Amboy (New Jersey) School District.

> **Box 4.4**
> # HIGHLIGHTS FROM A PREKINDERGARTEN LESSON PLAN USING PrePS TO AUGMENT A THEME-BASED CURRICULUM

1. **Introducing the word *observation.*** "I observe that you are wearing blue pants. I observe that our classroom is very quiet" What do you think it means to observe?

2. Before starting apple activities, **provide experiences with each sense.** To get some idea of children's baseline knowledge, draw pictures related to each sense (e.g., an ear for hearing, a tongue for tasting) and ask children to describe what we do with each.

3. Do 1- or 2-day **activities that focus on each sense.** To think about ears and hearing, blindfold each child, play a musical instrument, and ask them to identify what they are hearing. To explore skin and sense of touch, feel classroom items (e.g., puppets, bristle blocks, plastic people) and ask children to describe how they feel. Use words like *soft, smooth, hard, rough,* and *bumpy.*

4. **Start the apple observation** activity during large-group instruction (see Activity 3.1).

5. **Introduce science journals** to be used during small-group instruction. "Science journals are what scientists use when they make discoveries and they are also used to record, write, and draw information. Our journals are going to be used when we are observing." Have each child choose a journal and decorate the cover to make it recognizable as their own. After recording in journals, help children focus on the recording purpose (rather than creative drawing) of the science journal. Do this by noting color of drawing and asking if the apple the child observed is the same as the apple on the table. What's different/same about them?

6. **Start the apple prediction activity** (see Activity 3.2). During large-group instruction, discuss the observations made the day before. "Do you remember what we observed yesterday? What are some of the observations we made about the apple? Today we are going to predict what is inside the apple. Do you know what predict means? It is like guessing, we already know something about the apple. Now we are going to think and talk about what might be inside the apple." Record children's answers on chart paper. During small-group activity time, review each child's prediction. Take the opportunity to shape some of the predictions that were "not-as-good" guesses (e.g., large animals inside the apple). Have child observe the size of the apple then ask, "Is it *possible* for a [child's guess] to be inside this apple?" Also, ask children to think about prior relevant experience, "When you eat an apple, what is in there?" Have children draw their predictions and explain their drawings. Write down their descriptions. After they are finished, ask children how we could find out what is inside the apple. "What do we need to do to check the predictions?"

7. **Smelling apples: Compare apples and other fruits.** Discuss the activities from the previous 2 days. "On Monday, we used our senses to make observations about the apple. On Tuesday, we predicted what might be inside of the apple." Today we are going to explore how an apple smells. Use a piece of banana or orange and a slice of apple. Blindfold children and ask if they can tell which one is the apple using only their sense of smell (see Figure 4.8).

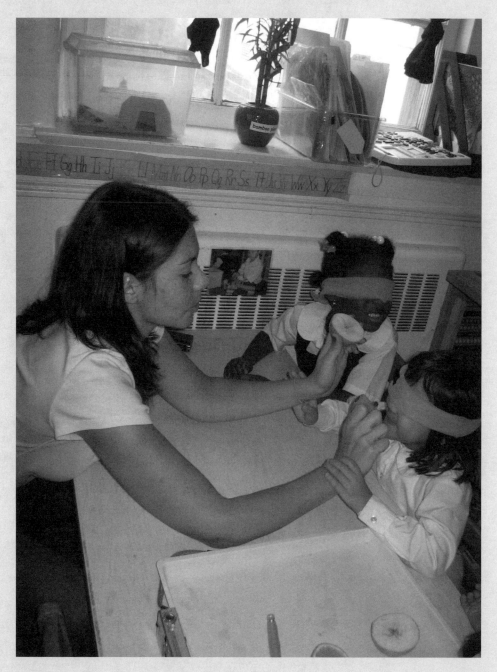

Figure 4.8.   What are you observing? Is it an apple or an orange?

8. **Using taste to explore apples.** Taste three different kinds of apples. Record children's observations of each. Then ask, "Which apple do you like best?" and record answers (see Figure 4.9 and Activity 4.1). Sing *I See Apples* (Jordano & Callella, 1998). Each color (red, yellow, green) is presented in a way that practices rhyming and phoneme blending.

9. **Using apples to introduce the balance scale.** Introduce a balance scale. Working in pairs, allow children to explore using apples and weights to play with the scale's movement. Then focus children's experiences. Demonstrate how to bal-

Gala Apple *How does the apple taste?*	**Granny Smith** *How does the apple taste?*	**Golden Delicious** *How does the apple taste?*
D: sweet C: juice K: it's juicy B: It's sweet K: it juicy W: taste like apple J: like apple Y: like fruit S: sabe, it taste like sour B: juicy	D: It taste like grass, so sour. C: It sour B: more sour K: It taste a lot of sour K: It's juicy sour T: it's sour W: blueberry J: sour G: it like sour Y: like lollipop, a green lollipop S: it's sour	D: They taste better these, the Gala. C: Sour B: Sour K: Sour, and taste a little bit sour K: it taste sour G: it taste like an apple, juicy W: it taste like a lollipop, purple. J: like a lollipop, it's sweet Y: it taste like watermelon T: like candy, like lollipop, sour B: like juicy S: like sour

Figure 4.9. Documenting apple tasting activities.

ance the scale using the weights on one side and the apple in the other. "Look at how the scale goes up and down. What does it mean when this side is down touching the floor and this side is up high?" Have them record the investigation in their journals (see Figure 4.10).

10. **Read *Five Red Apples*** (fingerplay by Kristen VanValkenberg, in Jordano & Callella, 1998). Have the children assist in the hand movements.

11. **Comparing and contrasting: Pears and apples.** Ask the children to identify the piece of fruit (pear). Ask them to tell you what they observe about the fruit. Record observations in journals. Also, record predictions for what is inside the pear. If necessary, remind them to think about the apple when predicting. "Will it be the same as the apple? Why do you think so? What will be the same? What might be different?" Later in the day (or the next day), check predictions.

12. **Experiment.** "Yesterday we observed a pear using our senses. Do you remember what we observed? Today we are going to observe the apples and the pears again. We are going to peel them and cut them up, like we did yesterday. What did we learn would happen to the apples and pears when we cut them? That's right. They turned brown. Today we are going to observe what happens if we put the apples and pears in water and in water with lemon juice. We'll leave some apples and pears alone. Let's predict what will happen to them. Do you think the ones we leave alone will turn brown? Why do you think so? Will they turn brown

Figure 4.10.   Recording what we found out about the balance scale.

in water? In water with lemon juice?" Use science journals. Have children discuss and record their observations of what is happening to the pears and the apples. Did any of the apples and pears stay white? Which ones? Did any of the apples and pears turn brown? Which ones?

13. **Make applesauce** (from apples we picked during a field trip to the orchard). Estimate how many apples are in the box. How can we check for sure? Check the number of apples in the box by counting. Recipe calls for 2 pounds of apples. "How can we measure 2 pounds of apples?" Weigh apples for the applesauce using a scale. Peel and remove the cores from the apples. "We are going to cook the apples. We will heat them. What do you predict will happen to the apples?" Cook the apples to check the predictions (and to make applesauce!).

14. **Begin pumpkin explorations.** First observe pumpkins. Have children identify the pumpkin and tell what they know about the pumpkin. Encourage them to use their observation skills. During journal time, encourage the children to look at the color and shape of the pumpkin before recording their observations. As they describe specific details they notice about the pumpkin, ask children how they think they could draw them.

15. **Make predictions about the inside of a pumpkin.** Discuss the observations made the day before. "Do you remember what was observed yesterday? What did we observe about the pumpkins? Let's check our chart. Today we are going to predict what is inside the pumpkin." Record answers on chart paper.

16. **Check what is inside the pumpkin.** Have children record their observations in their journals (see Figure 4.11).

17. **Weigh pumpkins.** Continue providing experience with the scales. Have children select the pumpkin that they think is the largest and heaviest and then smallest and lightest. "How can we find out?" Bring out scale and weigh the pumpkins that the children selected as the largest and smallest. Do you think another pumpkin might weigh less than this small pumpkin? How can we find out? Work on ideas of more and less with size and with weight. Use lots of comparative language. (Although size and weight aren't always correlated because different items have different densities, because we're using the same kind of things—pumpkins—the link between size and weight will be strong.)

   During small-group activities, continue math reasoning activities. Link the size of the pumpkin to its weight. Weigh a large pumpkin (9 or 10 pounds). Weigh a small pumpkin (2 pounds). Have children predict how much a medium-sized pumpkin will weigh. Shape their answers as needed. For example, if child says the medium pumpkin weighs 1 pound, review the size order: "Where's the smallest pumpkin? Where's the biggest pumpkin? What about this one? Right, it's in the middle. Now let's see. The smallest one weighs 2 pounds and the biggest one weighs 10 pounds. You predicted the middle-sized pumpkin will weigh 1 pound. That's *less* than the small pumpkin weighs. Do you think this one (medium) weighs less than this one (small)?" After child answers, "Let's check your prediction. Let's find out how much this one weighs."

Figure 4.11. Pumpkin explorations.

the school served a large number of Spanish-speaking families, which marked the first time that PrePS was used with classes of primarily English language learners.

Box 4.4 presents highlights from the teacher's own descriptions of, and notes about, her lesson plans with the prekindergarten class. Reading through these descriptions and notes, you will find that science practices are incorporated throughout the activities. This teacher successfully integrated important aspects of the PrePS approach into her teaching. As we began to introduce PrePS to more teachers, however, it became clear that not every teacher could so easily adopt the approach. For this reason, we developed the science practices planning grids (see Figure 3.12) and provided teachers with completed examples to illustrate typical PrePS learning experiences and the particular goals each meets. These are presented here.

Focusing on Individual Senses

After introducing observing, predicting, and checking using apples, a natural connection is to an in-depth exploration of senses. The central concept of form and function can be explored through a focus on senses and the particular kinds of information each provides for us. We have used this approach with documented successful outcomes for children's learning (see Chapter 5). Box 4.5 describes a proposed sequence

---

Box 4.5
EXPLORING OUR SENSES

1. **Observing apples using senses** (see Activity 3.1)

2. **Predicting and checking: What's inside the apple?** (see Activity 3.2)

3. **Comparing and contrasting apple varieties** (see Activity 4.1)

4. **More opportunities to observe, predict, and check.** If you think your students would benefit from more opportunities to practice the new vocabulary and procedures, feel free to repeat the activities using different objects. One twist on this activity is to have children observe real fruits and vegetables and inexpensive replicas (from a discount store), and then compare and contrast them. This highlights the differences in the substances that compose the objects. Children are really quite good at paying attention to this feature when it is the key distinguishing feature between two objects.

5. **Observing a coconut using all of the senses** (see Activity 4.2)

6. **Matching sounds** (see Activity 4.3)

7. **Touch and temperature.** In this activity, three seemingly identical items (two sealed containers filled with warm water and one with cool or two warmed therapy pads and one cool) are presented. Children are told that one of them is not like the others, and their job is to figure out which one is different. Have children suggest and test their ideas. Be sure to link their findings about temperature differences to their skin. Our skin is a tool that allows us to feel when things are hot or cool. (See Box 4.1 for an extension of this activity.)

8. **Sense of taste.** Present two bowls of applesauce to the children (natural versus sweetened with extra sugar) and ask children to compare how the two bowls (and the applesauce in them) look, smell, feel, and weigh. They seem identical, but we still have not used our sense of taste to explore them. Each child gets a chance to taste the applesauce and to make observations about the experience. Another food item that can look similar but taste different is cheese, which children can taste and then chart their preferences, similar to the apples in Activity 4.1.

9. **Sense of smell.** Make a large batch of playdough. Divide the dough in half and add different kinds of extract (mint and lemon work well) to each half. Keep the dough in zippered plastic bags so that children can see, shake, and feel it, noting that the two bags are the same on all of these features. Someone will suggest smelling (or the teacher can if necessary). The "smell-dough" activity is also very popular for playtime. Another activity involves smell jars that allow children to observe, predict, and check their predictions. Allow children to smell but not see items with distinctive scents (e.g., soap, coffee beans, orange slices, chocolate) and ask them to predict what they are smelling. You can write down their ideas or, if you would like to incorporate journals, have examples of possible items available for children to see. Ask them to choose which item they smelled and draw their prediction in their journal. Then show the items so they can use their eyes to check predictions.

10. **Sense of sight.** Vision is the only sensory channel through which we can perceive color. This activity involves hiding items in a brown paper bag, then asking children to judge the color of the item inside. Use items that are shaped the same but come in a wide array of colors (e.g., wooden blocks, crayons). Hide one in a bag, then display the full range of colors of the items on a tray, as well as a range of a second kind of item. Ask a child to feel what is in the bag. Which kind of thing is it (e.g., a crayon or a block)? How do you know? (The child should describe the shape or the teacher can help the child do so.) Once we know what kind of item it is because we can feel it, the next question is: What color is it? Children (and adults!) often have trouble admitting that they are unsure of something, but this activity makes clear that shape and texture can be sensed by feeling the object, but to know what color something is, we need our eyes.

11. **Using science tools to extend the senses: Magnifiers** (see Box 3.3)

12. **Muscles and heaviness.** The Massey and Roth (2004) activity series goes beyond the five senses to include learning activities that involve muscles/felt weight. To start a discussion about how our muscles help us feel heaviness, we use identical-looking boxes (two stuffed with newspaper only and one filled with paper and heavy books). One box is different than the other two. Can we find out which one is different and how? As a follow-up activity during small group, you can give children the chance to observe more subtle differences by filling identical opaque containers with clay or nothing. This activity also allows children to think about the concepts and terms *full* and *empty* using felt weight rather than vision (e.g., as in cups of juice) to make the determination.

13. **Using science tools to extend the senses: Balance scales** (see Activity 4.4).

of activities, which builds from foundational activities into an exploration of the functions of senses and finally incorporates some science tools that extend the senses. The series combines successful learning activities from our own classrooms with some designed by Christine Massey and Zipora Roth (2004).[3]

Some of these examples are further described in Activities 4.1–4.4, which also include science practices planning grids. The grids provide details about the learning goal(s) of the activity, materials needed, and the procedure. The activity series is flexible, allowing the teacher to provide more experience with a particular skill or concept before continuing, which is why some optional activities are provided. A number of the learning experiences are meant to extend over more than one day. Teachers can identify stopping points based on their knowledge of their students and their own class schedule (i.e., half day versus full day). As always, take time to let children really explore materials and discuss ideas, as this is more important than getting through the activities in a preset amount of time.

We developed these four extended examples for several reasons:

1. To illustrate ways that we have used PrePS to bring a science focus to classrooms

2. To provide examples that you might use, as written or as a starting point for generating your own activities

3. To demonstrate that PrePS plays out in different ways depending on the teacher, the curriculum, and the learners involved—something that is expected and encouraged

TIME TO EXPLORE . . . AND EXPLORE SOME MORE

Although children naturally explore and wonder about the world around them, thinking and working scientifically is a new experience for them. They need time to develop and practice these skills. Because it takes time to truly explore a concept, the PrePS teacher provides lots of learning experiences that allow children to think about a big science idea and to practice scientific thinking skills. Teachers also provide ample time for children to explore and work. This is a critical feature of PrePS; learners of all ages need time and multiple opportunities to exercise and practice new skills and ideas. Despite their reputation for short attention spans, we have found that when preschoolers are truly interested in an activity they can and do spend large amounts of time concentrating, exploring, and learning.

When PrePS teachers provide this time, children often respond by becoming deeply involved in science learning activities and investigations. The exact nature of their involvement may not be exactly what the teacher anticipates, however (see Box 4.6). One of our earliest examples of this comes from our introduction of date stamps to children. We found that children needed to explore in their own way (stamping happily away on journal pages, on their hands, and sometimes on each other) before they were ready to use the stamps as intended. Preschoolers are more

---

[3] Massey and Roth (2004) have published a fully field-tested K–1 science curriculum, *Science for Developing Minds*. In recent years, Gelman and Brenneman have worked with Massey and Roth to design and implement conceptually connected science learning experiences and to assess learning. The activities described in Box 4.5 grew out of this collaboration to study preschoolers.

Box 4.6
UNEXPECTED DIRECTIONS

A PrePS class was investigating reversible changes, such as melting and freezing. The teacher introduced an ice experiment and asked children to predict whether ice would melt faster in the sun or shade. On a hot day in Los Angeles, the children were more interested in exploring how ice melted in their mouths and on their skin. The teacher was sensitive to the children's need to play and investigate, so she encouraged them to do so. Eventually, the children finished their water play and were eager to participate in the planned experiment. In fact, the children were so engaged that they expanded their study to include different types of bowls (e.g., metal, plastic) to determine whether this factor affected melting.

likely to use measuring and observation tools appropriately once the tools become a familiar and regular part of the classroom environment. No teacher can be completely prepared for all the ways that children explore new materials. Instead, try to appreciate children's desire to become familiar with these new tools and to explore their possibilities before they are ready to proceed with your planned activities. When possible, keep supplies available during free time for further exploration so children have the opportunity to repeat an activity if they wish. Like rereading a story, repetition provides an opportunity to practice new knowledge, to explore new ideas, and to pick up more information.

The PrePS program stresses the need to repeatedly offer examples of an underlying concept and the importance of practicing while developing critical thinking skills. This repetition helps children to grasp a concept and to apply new knowledge to related activities or problems. The PrePS framework provides a structure for science activities so that each activity both builds on what came before and lays groundwork for what will follow. When children take the lead in exploring, it shows that they are thinking scientifically and making conceptual connections.

Exploring the Functions of Senses
COMPARING AND CONTRASTING WITH APPLES

This activity allows children to continue making careful observations by extending Activity 3.1/3.2. Children will engage in a tasting so that they can make different kinds of observations about apples. They also will practice comparing and contrasting two objects by describing what is the same and what is different about two types of apples.

PROCEDURE

Before class, make two charts with a photo or drawing of a Red Delicious apple (or first variety) on one side and the Granny Smith apple (or second variety) on the other. On one of the charts, transfer children's observations from Activity 3.1 of the outside of the red apple. Use this chart to review what children observed about that apple. (You will use the second chart later.) Then introduce the second type of apple. Ask children to observe this apple, too. Record their observations of this apple under its picture.(Learning the names of the different varieties of apples is less important than comparing and contrasting their features, although you can teach children the names if you like.)

MATERIALS

- At least two different types of apples that vary in color, shape, and/or size; use the same kind of apple that you used in Activity 3.1 (e.g., Red Delicious) and one that tastes very different (e.g., Granny Smith or another tart variety).

- Knife and cutting board

- Bowls or plates for sliced apples

- Posterboard for chart

If children are attentive, move on to a discussion of what is the same and what is different about the two apples. (Otherwise, wait until another circle time.) Eventually, children will be quite good at doing this—especially listing differences—but in this first activity, you should guide the discussion. You might start by stating something that is the same about the apples (e.g., "I observe that they both have a peel on the outside"). Then say that they are different in many ways, too. Ask the children about color of the apples: Is it the same or different? Continue in this way. If children make observations (written on the chart) that are the same for the two apples, be sure to point this out (e.g., "Oh, I see on our chart that José noticed that the red apple has a stem. Sara observed that the green apple has a stem, too. That is something that is the same about these apples. They have stems.").

Finally, ask the students to review what they observed inside the red apple. Do they predict that the green apple will be wet? Have seeds? Look white? How should they check those predictions? Cut open the green apple and compare the insides.

Dear _____,
This is a picture of my favorite kind of apple:

If you buy apples at the store, please get _____ apples. Thanks!
Love,

Figure A4.1   Example of apple letters.

91

Let children know that they will be eating the apples at snack time. This will give them a chance to use their tongues to taste the apples and to make new observations about them.

Snack Time

Tasting can be done at snack time. Refer to the observation charts to review the ways children already explored the apple (with their eyes and skin and perhaps muscles and noses). Allow children to try each apple and to describe the taste (and smell) of each. They might also want to describe how it feels to bite into each apple and to chew it. Are both apples crunchy? Maybe one is crunchier than the other? Add these observations to the observation chart.

To provide some experience with math and collecting data, have each child vote for the apple they like best. Use the second apple chart (prepared earlier) to collect the data. Have children write their names (or place a sticker with their name on it) under a picture of their favorite apple. The chart can be used to count and use comparative language (e.g., "Do more children like red apples or green apples?" "Which apple did James like better?").

An optional extension of this activity highlights literacy. After all children have tasted each apple and chosen a favorite, they can write a letter to their parents asking them to buy the kind of apple they liked best (see Figure A4.1). You can actually provide the letter, but the children are responsible for drawing a picture of their favorite. To do so, the children must pay attention to, and accurately record, the color of their favorite apple so that their parents know which kind of apples to buy at the store. This activity provides a clear purpose for recording accurately and helps to support children's growing awareness that writing and drawing can be used to communicate information.

SCIENCE PRACTICES PLANNING GRID: Activity 4.1

SCIENCE PRACTICE	*Concept/focus:* Form and function/senses *Experience:* Introduction to comparing and contrasting with apples using eyesight, touch, and taste
OBSERVE, PREDICT, CHECK	Children will make focused observations of different types of apples. The teacher records the children's observations on a chart that includes observations of both kinds of apples. After reviewing their observations of the inside of the first (red) apple, children can predict what they will find inside the second (green) apple.
COMPARE, CONTRAST, EXPERIMENT	The teacher guides children to notice how the apples are similar and how they are different. Similarities might include stems, having a peel, having seeds inside, and looking white inside. Differences might include skin color, shape, and size, but will depend on the type of apples chosen. Children will contrast the taste of the apples (sweet versus sour or tart).
VOCABULARY, DISCOURSE, LANGUAGE	Children will practice using the words *same* and *different* in context. Children will review some of the descriptive terms (e.g., *smooth, round, juicy*) and part names (e.g., *stem, seeds*) introduced in previous apple activities. Vocabulary to describe flavors (e.g., *sweet, sour, tart*) and food textures (such as *crunchy, crisp, mushy*) can be introduced.
COUNTING, MEASUREMENT, AND MATH	If children collect data on the class's favorite apples, the votes can be counted and compared.
RECORDING AND DOCUMENTING	The function of writing will be emphasized as the teacher records children's ideas on charts and uses the charts to recall information from past activities. The chart of the children's favorite apples introduces the idea of recording numerical information (simple data) on a chart. Using words and pictures to write a "favorite apple" letter to parents emphasizes that writing and drawing can be used to communicate.

Exploring the Functions of Senses
DESCRIBING COCONUTS

This activity provides children with more practice observing and describing objects. The main idea of this activity is that we can make many different observations about the same object or event. Children will describe a coconut and practice linking each of their observations to a particular sense. A coconut is just one way to give children this opportunity. Any object or event that involves multiple senses could be used.

PROCEDURE

Although it would be great to have children watch as you crack open a coconut, for safety reasons, you might want to do this before class. Use a screwdriver and hammer or a drill to make holes in the bottom of the coconut to drain milk from it. Use the hammer to crack the drained coconut. Using a vegetable peeler or a paring knife, remove some of the white meat from the shell so that children who want to do so can make observations about the taste of the coconut. Save the milk so children can see what was inside the coconut. If possible, take photos of each step of the process.

MATERIALS

- Two fresh coconuts (one whole and one that is cracked open)
- Screwdriver, hammer, and/or drill for draining and cracking
- Vegetable peeler or paring knife
- Posterboard for chart

Prepare a chart that has pictures of each sense across the top. You will write children's observations on this chart. In class (probably during group time), pass the coconut around and ask children what they notice about it. After they make an observation (e.g., "It is hairy"), ask them which sense or part of their body helped them to make that observation. (In this case, both skin and eyes help children make the observation that the coconut is hairy.) Once children have decided which sense helped them (or if they cannot, you can help them), write the observation under the corresponding sense picture(s).

Children will notice that they hear something inside the coconut and should be encouraged to describe what they think might be inside. Write down their predictions.

Show children the opened coconut and the milk you drained from it. Describe how you opened the coconut (use the pictures), and ask children to make observations about the inside of the coconut: What color is it? How does it feel? Does it have a smell? A few children will probably be willing to try eating the coconut meat. Allow them to taste the pieces you removed earlier and to describe their observations for the class.

During choice time or small-group time, children can record their observations of the coconut in their science journals. The teacher can also use this time to review the range of observations (using the chart made during the discussion) about the coconut and to ask children to (again) talk about which sense allowed them to find out that the coconut was, for example, "brown" or "made noise" or "smelled like dirt." This allows the teacher to assess children's understanding of new words and the kinds of information we get from each of our senses.

SCIENCE PRACTICES PLANNING GRID: Activity 4.2

SCIENCE PRACTICE	*Concept/focus:* Form and function/senses *Experience:* Making observations about a coconut
OBSERVE, PREDICT, CHECK	This activity allows children to make observations about the same object using multiple senses. Children will have the opportunity to predict what is inside of a coconut and how it will look and feel. They will check their predictions by observing the coconut opened by the teacher.
COMPARE, CONTRAST, EXPERIMENT	These practices are not the main focus of this activity.
VOCABULARY, DISCOURSE, LANGUAGE	The children and teacher will use varied vocabulary to describe their observations of the coconut. In the past, some children have spontaneously used similes to describe the smell (like grass, like dirt) and appearance (hairy like a lion) of the coconut. The teacher can encourage children to use more descriptive language of this sort (e.g., "Luis observes that the coconut smells. Does the smell remind you of anything you've smelled before?") and can model it as well (e.g., "Samiya observed that the coconut feels rough to her skin. I observed that, too. It reminds me of the bark of a tree.")
COUNTING, MEASUREMENT, AND MATH	These practices are not the main focus of this activity; however, the photos of the coconut cracking procedure can be used in a sequencing activity. Using the pictures, the teacher can ask children to choose and describe which picture comes first? What happens next? What does the coconut look like when we're finished cracking it?
RECORDING AND DOCUMENTING	The teacher will record children's observations of the coconut on a chart. Children's predictions about the inside of the coconut can also be recorded. The chart can be used to review vocabulary during small group time and/or during the next circle time. Children can record their observations of the coconut in their science journals.

Exploring the Functions of Senses
MATCHING SOUNDS

In this game, children are asked to find matches among items that look, smell, and feel the same but differ in one important way. Hearing is the sense that will help them find the match.[1]

PROCEDURE

Tell children that you have two containers. They must determine whether the containers are filled with the same thing, but they cannot open the containers to look. How will they figure out if the containers have the same stuff inside? They will need to use their other senses to observe the containers. (You should begin the activity with two containers that do not have the same filler. Matches will be introduced later in the activity.)

Ask children for their ideas. If they cannot come up with anything to try, review the senses and ask students whether they think any of their other senses will help them solve the problem. It probably will not be long until someone suggests using hearing. You then can say something such as, "Well, I'm using my ears, and I don't hear anything" to get children to suggest shaking the containers. When someone does, shake one container, then the other. Do the sounds match? (They should sound different.)

Now introduce another shaker. How does it sound? Ask children to observe carefully. Does the sound of this shaker match one of the others? Have another child shake this container. Does it have the same stuff inside as one of the other containers?

Sum up your findings so far by stating, "We used our ears to find out something about these containers. When you shake them, these two sound the same and this one sounds different." Ask the children how we can find out for sure whether "these two [the ones that sound the same] have the same stuff inside." The children should suggest looking inside (although some might remember the "no peeking" rule). Tell the children that now that they've solved the problem, they can open the containers. Their eyes will help them check for sure which containers have the same thing inside.

As a follow-up activity during small group, allow children to explore and match some of the other shakers you made. If you have extra containers, children might enjoy making some shakers themselves and playing the match game with you and their friends. Take the game outside and encourage children to use things from the play yard (sand from the sandbox, larger pebbles that are mixed into the sand, dirt, wood chips, and so on) to make shakers.

MATERIALS

- Shakers (e.g., old film canisters with lids; small, opaque plastic storage containers)

- Filler items that sound different when shaken (e.g., pennies, paper clips, sugar or sand, rice, dried beans)

- For the large-group activity, you will only need two kinds of shakers. However, you might want to make more for the children to explore later.

---

[1]This activity, like some others in this lesson series, is based on Massey and Roth (2004) activities in which the teacher sets up a problem—find the matches or determine which of three things is not like the others—in such a way that only one sense can solve it. This highlights the specific capabilities of individual senses.

SCIENCE PRACTICES PLANNING GRID: Activity 4.3

SCIENCE PRACTICE		*Concept/focus:* Form and function/senses *Experience:* Matching sounds using hearing
OBSERVE, PREDICT, CHECK		Children use their senses to explore seemingly identical containers. Using a particular sense (hearing), they are able to solve a problem and figure out which containers have the same stuff inside. They check the observations made with hearing by using their eyes.
COMPARE, CONTRAST, EXPERIMENT		Children compare and contrast containers using their senses. The containers look the same, smell the same, and even sound the same until they are shaken.
VOCABULARY, DISCOURSE, LANGUAGE		The terms same and different are used throughout the activity and are linked to specific features of the containers (e.g., same color, same shape, different sounds).
COUNTING, MEASUREMENT, AND MATH		These practices are not the main focus of this activity.
RECORDING AND DOCUMENTING		The teacher can use the senses chart (from Activity 4.2) to guide children's problem-solving activities.

Exploring the Functions of Senses
FELT WEIGHT AND BALANCE SCALES

This activity introduces balance scales in two interactive group time sessions that build on children's knowledge that they can use their muscles to tell which of two objects is heavier and links this knowledge to the balance scale.[1] Children are introduced to the balance scale as a tool that helps them tell which of two things is heavier, when it is not obvious just by holding the items. As children learned with magnifiers, sometimes their senses need help. Although understanding takes time and multiple experiences, this activity is an introduction to how to read the scale, how to balance it, and how to use it to determine which object (or set of objects) weighs more than another.

MATERIALS

- Balance scale
- Various heavy objects that will fit on the scale (e.g., paperweight, large rock)
- Various light objects that will fit on the scale (e.g., ping-pong ball, foam ball)
- Collection of items such as acorns, rocks, and shells
- Standard weight set for the balance scale

PROCEDURE

Start the activity by telling the children that you want to talk about things that are heavy and things that are light. Ask the children if they know what those words mean. You can ask them to name objects that weigh a lot and things that do not. Remind them that their muscles can help them find out how heavy things are.

Next, take a pair of objects that are obviously different in weight (e.g., a paperweight and a ping-pong ball). Have volunteers (or even the whole class) use their muscles to find out which one is heavier and ask them to report their findings to the group. Then tell the children that there is also a tool called a balance scale that can help us find out which thing weighs more. Put the two objects in the scale, and have children observe which side goes down. Emphasize that the heavier object made the balance scale go down. Repeat this with other objects of obviously different weights, having children judge felt weight and use the scale to find out which object is heavier.

Next, take two objects that are similar, but not equal, in weight. (You should test these objects on the scale beforehand to make sure that one is actually heavier.) Each child can hold the objects, then the children can vote to report which one they believe is heavier. There is likely to be a difference of opinion. Tell the children that sometimes their muscles cannot tell for sure which object is heavier, but the balance scale can help. Ask the children what the scale will do in response to the heavier object (go down). Check which is heavier by placing the objects in the scale. Repeat with different objects.

Finally (and this can be done at another time if children need a break), use two objects that are equal in weight. Have children use their muscles to try to figure out if the objects are differ-

---

[1] The balance scale activity was developed by Irena Nayfeld for her honors thesis when she worked in the Gelman Cognitive Development and Learning lab.

ent or the same. Ask them to think about what might happen to the scale if the objects weigh the same. Will one side go down? Then put the objects on the scale. Children will observe that the scale is even or balanced (neither side goes down). Ask the children what that means. Is one object heavier or do they weigh the same? Restate that objects that weigh the same will make the scale even (will balance the scale).

Within the next day or so, review the previous material. Ask children what they remember about the balance scale. What happens when they put a heavy object on one side and a light one on the other? What happens if they weigh the same? Take time to allow them to respond to these questions and to get ideas from multiple children. If the children seem interested or if their answers suggest they need to review, briefly repeat some of the activities.

You can use collections of items such as acorns, rocks, or shells to make the scale uneven. Then ask the children how they can make the other side (the lighter side) go down. What can they do to make that side heavier? For example, if you're using acorns and rocks, ask children to predict how many acorns it would take to make the lighter side go down. Do this several times with different amounts of items. You can have children put in the items and have the class count along. If you would like to explore making the scale balanced, it is best to use standard weights because one set of five acorns or shells might not weigh exactly the same as another set of five.

Encourage children to explore the balance scale further in the science area during free play by using different items or toys. Support their learning by asking questions that encourage them to interpret the position of the scale or to predict what will happen if you add to or take away items from one side.

SCIENCE PRACTICES PLANNING GRID: Activity 4.4

SCIENCE PRACTICE	*Concept/focus:* Form and function/senses *Experience:* Using the balance scale to weigh objects
OBSERVE, PREDICT, CHECK	Children observe objects with their muscles and then use the balance scale to extend their observations. Predictions are made about which side will go down when the objects are placed in the scale. Children check their observations and predictions about weight by placing the items in the scale.
COMPARE, CONTRAST, EXPERIMENT	Children compare and contrast different objects to find out which weigh more and compare sides of the scale to determine which has the heavier object. The activity allows children to conduct simple tests. They make observations and predictions and then test the predictions using a scientific tool.
VOCABULARY, DISCOURSE, LANGUAGE	The activity allows for discussion using comparison terms such as *heavier, lighter,* and *equal.* Related vocabulary such as *weight* and *balance* is used also, and children are taught the name of the tool (*balance scale*).
COUNTING, MEASUREMENT, AND MATH	Children are asked to think about the number of items that are needed to make one side heavier and/or balance the scale. As predictions are tested, children count the number of objects that it takes to achieve the task.
RECORDING AND DOCUMENTING	This science practice is not the focus of this activity; however, children can make journal entries that show the balance scale and items in it. (Figure 4.10 shows a child making an entry in his science journal as he explores the balance scale and weights. His teacher transcribed what he had to say about the entry.)

5

Assessment

Whether you use Preschool Pathways to Science (PrePS™) to plan your own comprehensive curriculum or as a way to enhance the science and math offerings of another curriculum, the program supports children's social, emotional, motor, and cognitive development. When you use the PrePS approach to plan a comprehensive curriculum, it must encourage the growth of the whole child, just as any high-quality program does. As a science curriculum, PrePS should foster children's abilities to think, talk, and work scientifically. If you decide to use PrePS to support your curricular planning, you will want to monitor your own teaching and your students' learning. The information in this chapter will help you to assess the effectiveness of PrePS in your classroom.

HOW DO WE KNOW PrePS SUPPORTS DEVELOPMENT OF THE WHOLE CHILD?

Throughout this book, we have described PrePS as a science-centered program that supports children's growth in other areas including, math, language and literacy, and socioemotional skills. We know that PrePS can be the foundation of a high-quality, comprehensive preschool program because of the success we have had at University of California, Los Angeles (UCLA) Early Care and Education. There are clear indices that point to the overall quality of the program.

UCLA Early Care and Education has been accredited by the National Association for the Education of Young Children (NAEYC) since the mid-1990s, the time frame that spans the introduction of PrePS. Achieving this distinction requires that a program volunteer to be measured on comprehensive and rigorous standards for the education, health, and safety of young children. The school has been recognized as an exemplary campus-based program by the HighScope Educational Research Foundation and by NAEYC. As part of a university with a graduate school of education, the school is often used as a site for the development of measures of classroom and instructional quality. The school's involvement exemplifies UCLA Early Care and Education's commitment to research that improves education for all children.

The UCLA Early Care and Education site was used to train assessors for the Classroom Assessment Learning System™ (CLASS™; Pianta, La Paro, & Hamre, 2008), which measures the quality of teacher–student interactions. The assessors noted that the school scored considerably higher than other programs on measures of instructional quality (Sharon Ritchie, personal communication, March 9, 2009). Although we cannot be certain, it seems reasonable that the school's emphasis on science supports extended, interactive conversations that yield high scores. The teaching at the school emphasizes encouraging teachers to asking open-ended questions and provide attentive, thoughtful responses to children's questions.

In addition, the school is part of the California Title V program. Self-study is required, and an external evaluation using the Early Childhood Environment Rating Scale–Revised Edition (ECERS-R; Harms, Clifford, & Cryer, 2007) is completed regularly by the California Department of Education. High scores on the various subscales of the ECERS-R are taken as evidence of a program's overall quality and potential for supporting children's learning and development. Curriculum and approach to teaching are just two factors that contribute to program quality; NAEYC (2006) lists eight other Early Childhood Program Standards: positive relationships, ongoing assessment of child progress, nutrition and health, teaching staff, relationships with families, community relationships, physical environment, and leadership and management that support high-quality service. Still, solid curriculum and teaching are necessary to achieve program excellence. The PrePS approach to curriculum, implementation, and teaching contributes to the exemplary program at UCLA Early Care and Education.

> As part of our work with the National Center for Early Childhood Education, NAEYC, National Institute for Early Education Research (NIEER), First 5, and our Los Angeles Community Partnerships, the UCLA Center for Improving Child Care Quality has been fortunate to use classrooms at the UCLA Early Child Care and Education program to develop measures of classroom learning environments and to train researchers to collect standardized measures of classroom child care quality. In the course of these activities over the last decade, we have collected classroom-level scores using the CLASS™, the ECERS-R, the Adult Involvement Scale (Howes & Stewart, 1987), and the Emerging Academics Snapshot (Ritchie, Howes, Kraft-Sayre, & Weiser, 2002). While institutional review board (IRB) human subject stipulations dictate that we will not release individual scores on these classrooms, I have reviewed them. All of the UCLA classroom scores indicate high-quality classroom environments, falling into the good to excellent end of the rated continuum. (Carollee Howes, personal communication, April 13, 2009)

HOW DO WE KNOW PrePS SUPPORTS SCIENTIFIC THINKING AND UNDERSTANDING?

While many assessments of the general quality of early childhood environments exist, tools to evaluate the instructional supports for preschool *science* are rare—perhaps because of the relative novelty of the idea that preschoolers can and do engage in scientific activities. As educators and policymakers commit themselves to providing early science learning experiences for children, assessment tools will be developed. We know of research teams who are currently working on this issue. Also, an extension of the ECERS scale (ECERS-E) already has been published (Sylva, Siraj-

Blatchford, & Taggart, 2006); it includes a subscale that assesses classroom materials and instructional supports for science, along with scales for literacy, mathematics, and diversity.

Although PrePS classrooms have not been evaluated using the ECERS-E, many of its indicators of high quality are present in our classrooms, including encouragement of children to explore natural phenomena and to make observations of these, perhaps by drawing them; provision of a wide range of science tools and reference materials, such as books and charts; and opportunities for children to discuss, ask questions, and record results of investigations. We were gratified to hear from one of our partner teachers in New Jersey that an ECERS-R evaluator began her report by noting the consistent use of math and science throughout the day in her classroom. Research tells us that math and science simply do not happen in many early childhood settings (Brenneman, Stevenson-Boyd, & Frede, 2009). It is especially welcome to receive independent confirmation that experience with PrePS is related to increased instructional offerings in these critical areas.

Of course, the main reason to measure classroom quality is to identify the materials, classroom practices, teaching methods, and curricular content that best support children's learning. Measures of general classroom quality show moderate relationships to children's learning outcomes (e.g., Burchinal et al., 2008). One study that measured relationships between mathematics and science environments (as measured by the ECERS-E) and learning suggested that higher science environment ratings were related to higher nonverbal reasoning skills for children (Sylva et al., 2006), although this relationship was not statistically significant. Planned and sustained early science experiences that occur over the whole school year have been linked to improved vocabulary outcomes (French, 2004). Educational interventions to support preschool children's learning about science content (e.g., Massey & Roth, 2009; Solomon & Johnson, 2000) and logical thinking skills (e.g., Klahr & Chen, 2003) have shown positive effects as well. Results like these suggest that well-designed science experiences support children's learning about science content and processes.

In recent years, with support from the National Science Foundation[1] we have been able to assess children's science learning as they participate in conceptually connected early science learning experiences. Data collection and analysis are ongoing, but the results are encouraging; connected learning experiences of the kind described in this book support children's growing understanding of science content and science practices. For example, we have given children repeated opportunities to run simple experiments. In a number of classes, these experiments involved sprouting seeds and growing plants. In others, the experiments tested the insulating properties of various materials such as feathers, knit scarves, and blubber (see Activity 3.3). At the end of the planned lessons, we asked children to generate their own simple tests. Children were asked to design a procedure to answer a "find-out" question (e.g., which of two kinds of gloves worked better to keep their hands warm). We compared our students with children who did not have the PrePS learning experiences. Children who had multiple opportunities to carry out simple experiments were more likely to design a test using one of each kind of glove (Brenneman et al., 2007; see Figure 5.1).

[1] The work reported here is funded by National Science Foundation Grant REC-0529579 awarded to R. Gelman, C. Massey, and K. Brenneman.

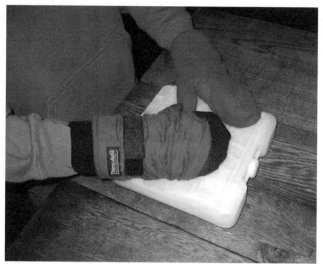

Figure 5.1. Simple experiments.

We also collected data from 44 4- and 5-year-old children before and after they had repeated experience doing simple experiments. We scored children's ability to interact with materials and to generate a simple procedure to test a question. The posttest revealed that 36 children's scores changed. Of these 75% improved and 25% did worse than they did on the pretest; thus, overall the intervention had a positive effect. Just as important, however, is that the procedure allowed us to assess the understandings of *individual* learners. We note that while children tended to improve, many did not master the skill. In the classroom, teachers can use information of this sort to make informed instructional decisions. These results show that young children benefit and learn from repeated classroom opportunities to answer questions by designing, running, and discussing simple experiments with their teachers and classmates (Brenneman & Gelman, 2009), but we also know that it is necessary to continue to provide more experience on the nature of an experiment. The important lesson is that it is possible to introduce the notion of an experiment to young children and place them on a relevant learning path for this important way of doing science and building knowledge.

As part of the NSF-funded team, we have tested the effectiveness of learning activities that focus on senses (Brenneman, Massey, & Metz, 2009) as well as growth and life cycles (Downs, Brenneman, Gelman, Massey, Nayfeld, & Roth, 2009), both of which are popular themes for preschool classrooms. We added educational power to activities by carefully designing learning experiences that build on each other and that incorporate key science practices.

As described in Chapter 4, we often introduce the idea that we use our senses as tools for observation early in the school year. This gives children the chance to practice and explore the various ways they can observe the world, and gets them thinking about the particular kinds of information they can get using each sense. In one small-scale (two classrooms) study of 3- and 4-year-olds, most of whom were English language learners, we found clear differences between children who had participated in a series of coherent activities that focused on their senses and making observations and those who had not. At the beginning of the school year, neither group could answer basic questions (asked in their dominant language) about the functions of their senses. The children whose teacher used the PrePS approach were better able match senses with their functions at post-test (79% of learners versus 27% in the comparison classroom); more PrePS children knew, for example, that they hear with their ears and do not taste with their eyes (see Figure 5.2). Similar positive results come from a larger study in which we assessed 4-year-old children's knowledge before and after participating in a learning series like that described in Box 4.5.

Finally, with older children (a class of 10 4- and 5-year-olds) from a university-based preschool classroom, we have moved children farther along the learning pathway for understanding that senses are tools for observation and, therefore, a means to build knowledge. After participation, this group could go beyond identifying the function of each sense to accurately judge the capabilities and limits of each sense in a problem-solving situation. Taken together, these studies support the PrePS approach of providing learning opportunities that converge on a common concept to build and extend children's understanding of important science ideas. The appreciation of what it means to make an observation is fundamental to the scientific method.

In another set of studies, we investigated children's knowledge about growth and life cycles before and after they participated in learning experiences designed to help them construct knowledge about these concepts. Recall from earlier chapters that developmental research indicates that children know a lot about the differences between animate and inanimate objects (see Activity 3.4). They know that animals can move by themselves but artifacts cannot. They expect the two kinds of things to be made of different "stuff" and to have different things inside of them. Animals have "blood, bones, and food" inside. Statues and machines have "wires, nothing,

Figure 5.2. Senses and observations.

and batteries" inside (e.g., Gelman, Spelke, & Meck, 1983). Children know that animals get hurt but artifacts break. They know that animals heal but artifacts need to be fixed by people (Backscheider, Shatz, & Gelman, 1993).

However, preschoolers have a somewhat harder time thinking about and talking about plants as members, along with animals, of the overarching category, living things (Carey, 1985). Plants are alive like animals. They grow like animals do, but they do not move around by themselves like animals can. We, therefore, designed a series of activities to support children's growing awareness of the similarities between plants and animals: that they both are alive, have life cycles, have parents and offspring, and have similar needs (e.g., nutrients, sunlight, water). We focused on comparing the two kinds of entities, but there are opportunities to contrast plants and animals as well; for example, they both need nutrients but get these in very different ways. Children's knowledge of plant and animal life cycles, and parent–offspring relations benefited from our in-class learning experiences (Downs et al., 2009). We assessed children's understanding that the offspring of a given species will be of the same species (e.g., a cat will have kittens, not puppies; the seeds from a bean plant will grow into a bean plant, not a palm tree) both before and after children participated in 8 weeks of conceptually connected learning experiences. Children more accurately predicted what would result from a bean seed (bean sprout) and a moth egg (caterpillar) after participation. They were also better at choosing what that item (sprout or caterpillar) would turn into (bean plant or moth). Among our 4- and 5-year-old students, two children received the same score before and after the learning experiences. Of the remaining 32 children, 84% improved. Again, these results tell us that the educational experiences we offer are related to gains in understanding, and they also help us determine which children will require more experience with the concepts and skills in question.

Our goal for PrePS is to offer experiences that build on the foundational competencies and curiosity that children already have to support further learning. Note that we are not expecting mastery by all students, nor are we expecting perfect performance on assessments, because individuals are at different points in their learning. Instead, our goal is improvement, and results from our studies indicate that we can meet this goal. Conceptually connected learning experiences put many children on science learning paths and move others farther along paths they are already on (Gelman, Romo, & Francis, 2002).

HOW CAN TEACHERS ASSESS THE EFFECTS OF PrePS ON THE CLASSROOM ENVIRONMENT AND ON STUDENTS' LEARNING?

Whether you decide to use the PrePS approach to plan a comprehensive curriculum (as we do at UCLA Early Care and Education) or as an add-on to another curriculum (as we have done in New Jersey schools), you will want to assess its usefulness and effectiveness. Assessment in preschool often relies on teachers' own observation and recording skills and on children's work products. Many teachers already write daily reports on classroom activities or individual children's behavior. Many also compile portfolios of children's work to chart progress over time. One way that

PrePS helps teachers to assess children's learning is by providing a wealth of information relevant to these efforts.

In any educational situation, a key question is whether children are learning what the teaching staff hopes they will learn. To answer this question, a teacher should have a clear educational goal and then seek data that indicate whether this goal is being met. Major sources of information are children's conversations with peers, teachers, and parents, and even their self-directed talk. For example, while watering the garden, a 4-year-old child remarked to the center director, "Plants need water to grow like me. You may be wondering why I put water on the ground when it needs to go all the way up into the plant, but it's sort of like a plant muscle. See my muscle [flexes arm]? The plant can pump the water up, up, up from the ground." This child is clearly trying to make connections between knowledge he has about muscles and something he is trying to understand about how water reaches the leaves in a plant. Conversations such as this could be followed up with learning experiences that allow the child to construct more complete and accurate understandings.

The activities children choose during free time can also indicate that they are thinking about science concepts and making connections, even when teachers are not guiding them to do so. The snake-measuring activity in Box 3.6 was designed by children during free play. Another example involves a 4-year-old girl who had been learning about insides and outsides. When she found a small, round, green object on the playground, she wanted the class to talk about what it might be. During circle time, the class discussed the object and proposed investigations to test their ideas. Cutting it open or planting it (because many children believed that it was a seed) were mentioned. Later, two children independently collected 30 more of the mysterious green objects, enough for every child to study. The children requested plates, knives, magnifying glasses, science journals, pens, and a date stamp to complete their investigation. After the materials were collected, the class spent some time exploring these mystery objects. Clearly, these children were motivated and able to use a scientific approach to seek answers to a question that interested them.

As we have discussed, PrePS experiences also support language growth. The teacher who is looking for evidence of children's vocabulary skills or ability to describe objects or events will find plenty in children's talk about science. We have reams of transcripts from large- and small-group conversations. These discussions reveal teachers' and students' use of new terms. A child who looks at a building block and tells the teacher, "It's blue. It's a rectangle. I cannot observe any more," clearly understands the meaning of the term *observe*. Journal entries are another source of information about the new vocabulary children are learning.

PrePS teachers of English language learners have been particularly excited about the ways that science conversations (in group time or one-on-one over journals) encourage children's use of descriptive language vocabulary and provide clear evidence of their learning progress. These conversations also inform teachers about children's use of more complex language. Making predictions and describing why something happened encourages the use of more complicated sentences (Gelman & Brenneman, in press). By engaging children in these ways, teachers not only provide learning opportunities, they also give children a chance to "show their stuff" in a meaningful context. This, in turn, provides teachers with evidence about children's language skills.

Chapter 3 introduced journals as supports for children's learning. These also serve as an assessment tool for teachers by providing information about children's thinking and skills across a wide range of curricular areas. When staff and children discuss the journal entries, teachers can probe conceptual understandings, assess vocabulary development, get evidence of language growth, assess fine motor skills, get a sense of a child's attention to detail, and look for evidence of preliteracy understandings (Brenneman & Louro, 2008). Discussing a child's journal entry is a formative assessment opportunity. It allows the teacher to ask, "What does this child already understand? Which questions can I ask or experiences can I provide to support further learning? Does this child have any misunderstandings? If so, what can I do to help replace these with understanding?"

Figure 5.3 shows a journal entry that reveals a possible misunderstanding. The child seems to believe that it is the number of seeds planted, rather than the medium into which they are planted, that affects sprouting of grass seed. While it is true that planting many seeds in a small space causes competition and reduces growth, this was not the case here. Even if it were, it is important for the child to think about the effects of soil and sand. Depending on the individual learner, the teacher might gently challenge the notion by saying, "I wonder if it's the number of the seeds? Maybe it's the sand? What do you think?" The teacher can then encourage the child to think of ways to find out for sure, "How could we find out for sure? Can we do a test? What should we do?" An experiment could be done to find out which factor affects growth. This journal entry is also notable for the child's use of causal language as she explains the results of her experiment.

Journals also provide opportunities for summative assessment at the end of a unit or at the end of a term (Gelman et al., 2002). For example, as part of explorations of the central concept (and subcategory) change through growth, children participated in a number of experiences designed to support their understanding of the plant life cycle. To find out for sure whether plants need water and sun to grow, we planted seeds under a number of conditions: with sun and water, with sun but no water, with water but no sun, and with neither sun nor water.[2] We observed and described the

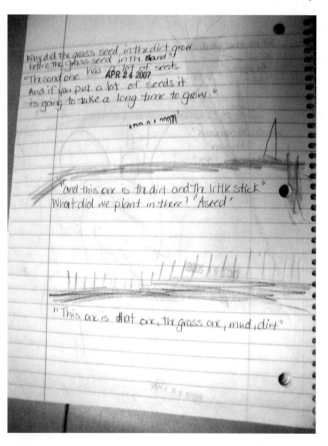

Figure 5.3.   Journal page showing a possible misconception.

_____

[2] In subsequent years, we have kept the variables of sun and water separate. That is, in one set of activities, we contrast plants grown in the sun or not (but both watered). In another, we explore the effects of water by growing all plants in sun but by watering only half of them. Doing the experiments this way makes clearer to children which factors are affecting the plants.

plants as they grew. After a number of weeks, we discussed the characteristics of plants that were grown in the closet, without sunlight. Children were surprised that the plants in the closet grew at all. Not only that, they had very long stems—even longer than the stems on the plants grown with water and sunlight! Children also noticed, though, that the bean plants given water and sun were a darker green, had more leaves, had bigger leaves, and were standing up straight. They looked much healthier than the plants grown in the dark without water. Children then journaled the results of the experiment; many of them accurately recorded key differences between the two kinds of plants (see Figure 5.4). In and of themselves, these entries provide a wealth of information about children's attention to detail and use of descriptive language.

Journal entries also can be revisited with the children to find out how much they remember about an investigation. The entries serve as reminders of a past event. With the healthy and unhealthy bean plant entries, we asked each child to discuss their journal page with an adult from outside the classroom, including what differences were found between the plants, which plants were healthy, and how children knew this. In this way, the journals provided a way to assess how much information children retained over time. Teachers can revisit entries with children to find out what they remember and to assess whether their descriptions get more sophisticated conceptually or linguistically as the year progresses.

Journals provide a permanent, dated record of children's work throughout the year. Contrasting entries from the beginning of the year with ones from the end provides dramatic evidence for changes in children's fine motor skills, attention to detail, and ability to describe what they have drawn using varied vocabulary and more complex sentences. Especially for older children, the journals might also document children's growing writing skills. Some children begin to want to label items for themselves by using invented spelling, asking teachers for help spelling, or using an adult's writing as a model. These advances in preliteracy will be reflected in the journal entries over the year.

Changes in the use of journals across the year also are a marker of development in children's understanding of the purpose of this tool itself. As the year progresses, do more of the entries reflect science content (rather than purely creative drawings)? Do children remember to date their work? Do they decrease the use of multiple date stamps, showing that they are treating the stamp less as an art tool and more as a sci-

Figure 5.4. Bean plant journals.

ence tool? Figure 1.1 in Chapter 1 is an example of the changes indicating that children's skills and ideas are progressing. In addition to inferring children's understandings from their entries, you can ask children directly about the functions of journals and date stamps. The conversation in Box 5.1 occurred spontaneously, but you could enlist another adult to informally talk to the children in a similar way.

HOW DO I KNOW IF I'M DOING IT RIGHT?

PrePS was developed to support teachers as they encourage children to learn, do, and understand science. We have provided some evidence that the PrePS approach supports both a high-quality classroom learning environment generally and learning of science concepts and practices specifically. Children learn when they are encouraged to think deeply about the same concept or idea through multiple activities and experiences. Beyond research findings and scores, we also have the thoughts and opinions of the teachers who have worked with us and with PrePS. Many report changes in their teaching approach and attitudes toward science.

Box 5.1
A CONVERSATION ABOUT SCIENCE JOURNALS

A few months into the school year, an adult who was not a regular visitor to the classroom (but who was familiar with PrePS) asked two children, Marco and Brianna, about the rack of science journals.

Adult: What are those things?

Brianna: Those are our science journals.

Adult: What are science journals?

Marco: They're where we write stuff, experiments.

Brianna: Uh-huh, and draw pictures.

Adult: Can you show me? [points to the date stamp on a journal entry] What's that?

Brianna: That's the date.

Marco: It's the date stamper.

Adult: Why did you put one on every page?

Brianna: So we know when we wrote it.

The three then sat together, and the children asked the adult to read the dates on each entry. The children were able to indicate which entries were written before or after others, even when these did not appear on adjacent pages. They used the stamped dates, rather than order of pages, to keep track of time.

...your program really helped me rethink how I treat science in the daily activities with the kids. I've realized now that I'm more comfortable with the science terms....Well, it's not so scary anymore.

—SL, New Jersey preschool teacher

For some teachers, adopting at least some aspects of PrePS is relatively easy. Other teachers find it helpful to use example lessons as models. By now, however, it should be clear that we do not believe that there is one *right* way to do PrePS. There isn't even one right way to lead a particular learning experience. This situation can be liberating or frustrating for teachers. In response to our experiences working alongside teachers, we have made quite a few changes to our own approach to introducing them to PrePS and supporting them as they use it. This book is the result of our self-assessments, in which we have retained what worked and retooled what needed improvement. We are certain that reactions, advice, criticisms, and (we hope) success stories from you will contribute to changes in future versions of this book.

Our point is that every one of us should take the time to reflect on what we are doing, what our goals are, and whether what we are doing is helping us to meet our goals effectively and efficiently. As a teacher, your best indications that PrePS is working will come from assessments of children's learning. Another great way to determine if you are getting into the spirit of PrePS is to look at your walls (see Box 5.2).

SOME FINAL THOUGHTS

We began developing PrePS many years ago. Since then, researchers, educators, and policymakers have turned more attention to science education in the early years. The National Research Council has focused on improving K–8 science by outlining relevant research (Duschl et al., 2006) and providing practical applications of that research for educators (Michaels, Shouse, & Schweingruber, 2008). Each volume also documents the wide range of foundational skills and content knowledge that young children bring to school when they enter kindergarten. At the same time, there has been a national push for better descriptions of what children should be learning in preschool. As of 2005, almost every state had written standards or learning expectations for early language, literacy, and mathematics (Neuman & Roskos, 2005). Most states have science learning expectations, too. For example, the New Jersey Department of Education outlines four expectations for science education in preschool (see Box 5.3). We are pleased that our long-held belief that science has an important place in preschool classrooms is being borne out.

Supporting young children as they develop scientific thinking skills and gain content knowledge is critical if they are to become scientifically literate members of society. Just as important is ensuring that teachers maintain the natural enthusiasm and curiosity children have about the world and the science in it. So often when we describe PrePS as a method for introducing preschoolers to science—helping them feel comfortable with the tools, methods, and content of the field—adults react with pure excitement. They tell us that their educational experiences with science were dry and difficult; they came away thinking that science had very little to do with everyday life. In that traditional classroom, students did not use science to answer their own questions or solve problems that mattered to them. Experiments were com-

Box 5.2
THE WALLS

Many preschool classrooms have posters that encourage children to "Read!" There are examples of children's artwork, and maybe bulletin boards created by teachers to draw attention to the week's topic of study. When PrePS is introduced, however, the walls change. Children's *ideas* are evident everywhere. Observation and prediction charts recording children's descriptions and explanations can be found hanging on the walls (see Figure 5.5). Children appreciate being able to review these throughout the day, often asking that a teacher read back "my prediction" during lunch or snack time. Alongside children's artistic creations are drawings about science explorations that reflect children's observations and understandings of a given concept. When we introduce PrePS to teachers, we ask them to think about the walls of their classroom. How much of what hangs there represents the ideas and thoughts of children? As teachers introduce scientific ways of thinking, talking, doing, and understanding, this answer is likely to change.

Figure 5.5.   Walls in a PrePS classroom.

Box 5.3
NEW JERSEY STATE DEPARTMENT OF EDUCATION PRESCHOOL TEACHING AND LEARNING EXPECTATIONS

Expectation 1: Children develop inquiry skills, including problem solving and decision making.

Expectation 2: Children observe and investigate the properties of objects, both living and nonliving.

Expectation 3: Children explore the concept of change in both living and nonliving entities and in the environment.

Expectation 4: Children develop an awareness of the environment and human responsibility for its care.

Retrieved March 2, 2009 from http://www.state.nj.us/education/ece/code/expectations/expectations.pdf

pleted to repeat the answers to questions others had already asked and investigated. The instructions were presented in steps, with no opportunity for creativity and no chance to explore an interesting idea. Facts were memorized and recalled, but with no sense of conceptual mastery.

The PrePS program does not guarantee mastery, but the feeling that one is capable of learning and doing science is fostered when science is viewed from an early age as an exciting part of everyday life. PrePS provides a foundation for this future learning by nurturing young children's natural curiosity about the world. The great potential of PrePS is that it puts children on learning paths for science. They know enough to be motivated to do, know, and discover more. The goal of PrePS is for children to know this joy of discovery—and, having known it, to desire it again and again.

References

Appelbaum, P., & Clark, S. (2001). Science! Fun? A critical analysis of design/content/evaluation. *Journal of Curriculum Studies, 33,* 583–600.

Backsheider, A.G., Shatz, M., & Gelman, S.A. (1993). Preschoolers' ability to distinguish living kinds as a function of regrowth. *Child Development, 64,* 1242–1257.

Baillargeon, R., Yu, D., Yuan, S., Li, J., & Luo, Y. (2009). Young infants' expectations about self-propelled objects. In B.M. Hood & L.R. Santos (Eds.), *The origins of object knowledge* (pp. 285–352). New York: Oxford University Press.

Bowman, B., Donovan, M.S., & Burns, M.S. (Eds.). (2001). *Eager to learn: Educating our preschoolers.* Washington, DC: National Academies Press.

Bransford, J.D., Brown, A.L., & Cocking, R. (Eds.). (1999). *How people learn: Brain, mind, experience, and school.* Washington, DC: National Academies Press.

Brenneman, K., & Gelman, R. (2009, April). *Supporting and assessing scientific reasoning in young children.* Presented at the biennial meeting of the Society for Researh in Child Development, Denver, CO.

Brenneman, K., Gelman, R., Massey, C., Roth, Z., Nayfeld, I., & Downs, L.E. (2007, October). *Preschool pathways to science: Assessing and fostering scientific reasoning in preschoolers.* Presented at the biennial meeting of the Cognitive Development Society, Santa Fe, NM.

Brenneman, K., & Louro, I.F. (2008). Science journals in the preschool classroom. *Early Childhood Education Journal, 36,* 113–119.

Brenneman, K., Massey, C., & Metz, K. (2009, April). *Science in the early childhood classroom: Introducing senses as tools for observation.* Presented at the biennial meeting of the Society for Research in Child Development, Denver, CO.

Brenneman, K., Stevenson-Boyd, J., & Frede, E.C. (2009, March). Math and science in preschool: Policies and practice. *NIEER Preschool Policy Brief, 19.* New Brunswick, NJ: National Institute for Early Education Research. Retrieved June 1, 2009, from http://nieer.org/resources/policybriefs/20.pdf

Brown, A.L., & Campione, J.C. (1996). Psychological theory and the design of innovative learning environments: On procedures, principles, and systems. In L. Schauble & R. Glaser (Eds.), *Contributions of instructional innovation to understanding theory* (pp. 229–270). Mahwah, NJ: Lawrence Erlbaum Associates.

Bruner, J.S. (1964). The course of cognitive growth. *American Psychologist, 19,* 1–15.

Bullock, M., & Gelman, R. (1979). Preschool children's assumptions about cause and effect: Temporal ordering. *Child Development, 50,* 89–96.

Burchinal, M., Howes, C., Pianta, R., Bryant, D., Early, D., Clifford, R., Barbarin, O. (2008). Predicting child outcomes at the end of kindergarten from the quality of pre-kindergarten teacher–child interactions and instruction. *Applied Developmental Science, 12,* 140–153.

Campbell, J. (2006). *Handbook of mathematical cognition.* London: Psychology Press.

Carey, S. (1985). *Conceptual change in childhood.* Cambridge, MA: The MIT Press.

Carey, S. (2009). *The origin of concepts.* New York: Oxford University Press.

Cheng, K., & Newcombe, N. (2005). Is there a geometric module for spatial orientation? Squaring theory and evidence. *Psychonomic Bulletin and Review, 12,* 1–23.

Chouinard, M.M. (2007). Children's questions: A mechanism for cognitive development. *Monographs of the Society for Research in Child Development, 72,* 1–129.

Conezio, K., & French, L. (2002). Science in the preschool classroom: Capitalizing on children's fascination with the everyday world to foster language and literacy development. *Young Children, 57,* 12–18.

Danby, S.J. (2002). The communicative competence of young children. *Australian Journal of Early Childhood, 27,* 25–30.

Dehaene, S., & Changeux, J. (1993). Development of elementary numerical abilities: A neuronal model. *Journal of Cognitive Neuroscience, 5,* 390–407.

Dickinson, D.K. (2001). Large-group and free-play times: Conversational settings supporting language and literacy development. In D.K. Dickinson & P.O. Tabors (Eds.), *Beginning literacy with language* (pp. 223–255). Baltimore: Paul H. Brookes Publishing Co.

Downs, L., Brenneman, K., Gelman, R., Massey, C., Nayfeld, I., & Roth, Z. (2009, April). *Developing classroom experiences to support preschoolers' knowledge of living things.* Presented at the biennial meeting of the Society for Research in Child Development, Denver, CO.

Dunbar, K., & Fugelsang, J. (2005). Scientific thinking and reasoning. In K. Holyoak & R.G. Morrison (Eds.), *The Cambridge handbook of thinking and reasoning* (pp. 706–726). New York: Cambridge University Press.

Duschl, R.A., Schweingruber, H.A., & Shouse, A.W. (2006). *Taking science to school: Learning and teaching science in grades K–8.* Washington, DC: National Academies Press.

Elkind, D. (1989). *The hurried child: Growing up too fast too soon.* Reading, MA: Addison-Wesley.

French, L. (2004). Science as the center of a coherent, integrated, early childhood curriculum. *Early Childhood Research Quarterly, 19,* 138–149.

Gallas, K. (1995). *Talking their way into science: Hearing children's questions and theories, responding with curricula.* New York: Teachers College Press.

Gallistel, C.R., & Gelman, R. (2005). Mathematical cognition. In K. Holyoak & R. Morrison (Eds.) *Cambridge handbook of thinking and reasoning* (pp. 559–588). New York: Cambridge University Press.

Gardner, H. (1991). *The unschooled mind: How children think and how schools should teach.* San Francisco: Basic Books.

Gelman, R. (1990). First principles organize attention to relevant data and the acquisition of numerical and causal concepts. *Cognitive Science, 14,* 79–106.

Gelman, R. (1998). Domain specificity in cognitive development: Universals and nonuniversals. In M. Sabourin & F. Craik (Eds.), *Advances in psychological science: Vol. 2. Biological and cognitive aspects* (pp. 557–579). Hove, England: Psychology Press.

Gelman, R. (2009). Innate learning and beyond. In M. Piattelli-Palmarini, P. Salaburu, & J. Uriagereka (Eds.), *Of minds and language: A dialogue with Noam Chomsky in the Basque country* (pp. 223–238). New York: Oxford University Press.

Gelman, R., & Baillargeon, R. (1983). A review of some Piagetian concepts. In J.H. Flavell & E. Markman (Eds.), *Cognitive development: Vol. 3. Handbook of child development* (pp. 167–230). New York: John Wiley & Sons.

Gelman, R., & Brenneman, K. (2004). Science learning pathways for young children. *Early Childhood Research Quarterly, 19,* 150–158.

Gelman, R., & Brenneman, K. (in press). Science classrooms as learning labs. In N. Stein & S. Raudenbusch (Eds.), *Developmental cognitive science goes to school.* New York: Taylor & Francis.

Gelman, R., & Gallistel, C.R. (1978). *The child's understanding of number.* Cambridge, MA: Harvard University Press.

Gelman, R. & Lucariello, J. (2002). Learning in cognitive development. In H. Pashler & C.R. Gallistel (Eds.), *Stevens' handbook of experimental psychology* (3rd ed., Vol. 3, pp. 395–443). New York: John Wiley & Sons.

Gelman, R., Romo, L., & Francis, W.S. (2002). Notebooks as windows on learning: The case of a science-into-ESL program. In N. Granott & J. Parziale (Eds.), *Microdevelopment: Transition processes in development and learning* (pp. 269–293). Cambridge, England: Cambridge University Press.

Gelman, R., & Shatz, M. (1977). Appropriate speech adjustments: The operation of conversational constraints on talk to two-year-olds. In M. Lewis & L. Rosenblum (Eds.), *Interaction, conversation and the development of language* (pp. 189–198). New York: John Wiley & Sons.

Gelman, R., Spelke, E.S., & Meck, E. (1983). What preschoolers know about animate and inanimate objects. In D. Rogers & J. Sloboda (Eds.), *The development of symbolic thought* (pp. 297–328). London: Plenum.

Gelman, R., & Williams, E. (1998). Enabling constraints for cognitive development and learning: Domain specificity and epigenesis. In W. Damon (Series Ed.) & D. Kuhn & R. Siegler (Vol. Eds.), *Handbook of child psychology: Vol. 2. Cognition, perception and language* (5th ed., pp. 575–630). New York: John Wiley & Sons.

Gelman, S.A. (2003). *The essential child: Origins of essentialism in everyday thought.* New York: Oxford University Press.

Gelman, S., & Markman, E. (1986). Categories and induction in young children. *Cognition, 23,* 183–209.

Gelman, S.A., & Opfer, J.E. (2002). Development of the animate–inanimate distinction. In U. Goswami (Ed.), *Blackwell handbook of childhood cognitive development* (pp. 151–166). Oxford: Blackwell.

Gentner, D. (2005). The development of relational category knowledge. In L. Gershkoff-Stowe & D.H. Rakison (Eds.), *Building object categories in developmental time* (pp. 245–275). Mahwah, NJ: Lawrence Erlbaum Associates.

Gibson, E.J. (1970). *Principles of perceptual learning and development.* New York: Appleton-Century-Crofts.

Ginsburg, H.P., Lee, J.S., & Boyd, J.S. (2008). Mathematics education for young children: What it is and how to promote it. *Society for Research in Child Development Social Policy Report, 22,* 3–22.

Gobbo, C., & Chi, M. (1986). How knowledge is structured and used by expert and novice children. *Cognitive Development, 1,* 221–237.

Gopnik, A., & Schulz, L. (Eds.). (2007). *Causal learning: Psychology, philosophy, computation.* New York: Oxford University Press.

Gottfried, G.M., & Gelman, S. (2004). Developing domain-specific causal–explanatory frameworks: The role of insides and immanence. *Cognitive Development, 20,* 137–158.

Hammer, D. (1999). Physics for first graders? *Science Education, 83,* 797–799.

Hart, B., & Risley, T.R. (1995). *Meaningful differences in the everyday experience of young American children.* Baltimore: Paul H. Brookes Publishing Co.

Harms, T., Clifford, R.M., & Cryer, D. (2007). *Early Childhood Environment Rating Scale–Revised Edition* (ECERS-R). New York: Teachers College Press.

Hermer, L., & Spelke, E.S. (1996). Modularity and development: The case of spatial reorientation. *Cognition, 61,* 195–232.

Hong, L.T. (1995). *The empress and the silkworm.* Morton Grove, IL: Albert Whitman and. Co.

Howes, C., & Stewart, P. (1987). Child's play with adults, toys, and peers: An examination of family and child-care influences. *Developmental Psychology, 23,* 423–430.

Inagaki, K., & Hatano, G. (2002). *Young children's naive thinking about the biological world.* New York: Psychology Press.

Inhelder, B., & Piaget, J. (1964). *The early growth of logic in the child: Classification and seriation.* London: Routledge and Kegan Paul.

Jordano, K., & Callella, T. (1998). *Phonemic awareness songs and rhymes.* Cypress, CA: Creative Teaching Press.

Kail, R.V. (2007). *Children and their development* (4th ed.). Upper Saddle River, NJ: Prentice Hall.

Karmiloff-Smith, A., & Inhelder, B. (1974). If you want to get ahead, get a theory. *Cognition, 3,* 195–212.

Klahr, D., & Chen, Z. (2003). Overcoming the positive-capture strategy in young children: Learning about indeterminacy. *Child Development, 74,* 1275–1296.

Kuhn, T.S. (1962). *The structure of scientific revolutions.* Chicago: University of Chicago Press.

Lavin, B., Galotti, K., & Gelman, R. (2003). *When children, not adults, are the experts: Explorations of a child-oriented environment.* Unpublished manuscript.

Lionni, L. (2006). *Alexander and the wind-up mouse.* New York: Knopf Books for Young Readers.

Macario, J. (1991). Young children's use of color classification: Foods and other canonically colored objects. *Cognitive Development, 6,* 17–46.

Massey, C., & Roth, Z. (2004). *Science for Developing Minds series: A science curriculum for kindergarten and first grade.* Philadelphia: Edventures.

Massey, C., & Roth, Z. (2009, April). *Conceptual change in preschool science: Understanding light and shadows.* Presented at the biennial meeting of the Society for Research in Child Development, Denver, CO.

McCloskey, M., Washburn, A., & Felch, L. (1983). Intuitive physics: The straight-down belief and its origin. *Journal of Experimental Psychology: Learning, Memory and Cognition, 9,* 636–649.

Michaels, S., Shouse, A.W., & Schweingruber, H.A. (2008). *Ready, set, science! Putting research to work in K–8 science classrooms.* Washington, DC: National Academies Press

Miller, G.A. (1977). *Spontaneous apprentices: Children and language.* New York: Seabury Press.

Munakata, Y. (2006). Information processing approaches to development. In W. Damon & R.M. Lerner (Series Eds.) & D. Kuhn & R. Siegler (Vol. Eds.), *Handbook of child psychology: Vol. 2. Cognition, perception, and language* (6th ed., pp. 426–463). Hoboken, NJ: John Wiley & Sons.

National Association for the Education of Young Children. (2006). *NAEYC develops 10 standards of high-quality early childhood education.* Retrieved March 9, 2009, from http://www.naeyc.org/about/releases/20060416.asp

National Science Board. (2009). *National Science Board STEM education recommendations for the President-Elect Obama administration.* Retrieved March 9, 2009, from http://www.nsf.gov/nsb/publications/2009/01_10_stem_rec_obama.pdf

Nayfeld, I., Brenneman, K., & Gelman, R. (2009, under review). *Science in the classroom: Finding a balance between autonomous exploration and teacher-led instruction in preschool settings.*

Neuman, S., & Roskos, K. (2005). The state of state pre-kindergarten standards. *Early Childhood Research Quarterly, 20,* 125–145.

Novak, J.D., & Gowin, D.B. (1984). *Learning how to learn.* New York: Cambridge University Press.

Perlmutter, M. (1980). *Children's memory.* San Francisco: Jossey-Bass.

Piaget, J. (1930). *The child's conception of physical causality.* London: Routledge & Kegan Paul.

Piaget, J. (1952). *The child's conception of number.* London: Routledge.

Piaget, J. (1970). Piaget's theory. In P.H. Mussen (Ed.), *Carmichael's manual of child psychology* (Vol. 1, pp. 103–128). New York: Wiley.

Pianta, R.C., La Paro, K.M., & Hamre, B.K. (2008). *Classroom Assessment Scoring System™ (CLASS™).* Baltimore: Paul H. Brookes Publishing Co.

Poulin-Dubois, D. (1999). Infants' distinction between animate and inanimate objects: The origins of naïve psychology. In P. Rochat (Ed.), *Early social cognition* (pp. 257–280). Mahwah, NJ: Lawrence Erlbaum Associates.

Resnick, L.B. (1987). *Education and learning to think.* Washington, DC: National Academies Press.

Ritchie, S., Howes, C., Kraft-Sayre, M., & Weiser, B. (2002). *Emergent academic snapshot.* Los Angeles: University of California.

Saxe, R., Tzelnic, T., & Carey, S. (2007). Knowing who-dunnit: Infants identify the causal agent in an unseen causal interaction. *Developmental Psychology, 43,* 149–158.

Schulz, L.E., & Bonawitz, E.B. (2007). Serious fun: Preschoolers engage in more exploratory play when evidence is confounded. *Developmental Psychology, 43,* 1045–1050.

Shatz, M., & Gelman, R. (1973). The development of communication skills: Modifications in the speech of young children as a function of listener. *Monographs of the Society for Research in Child Development, 38*(Serial No. 152), 1–37.

Siegal, M., & Surian, L. (2004). Conceptual development and conversational understanding. *Trends in Cognitive Sciences, 8,* 534–538.

Solomon, G.E.A., & Johnson, S.C. (2000). Conceptual change in the classroom: teaching young children to understand biological inheritance. *British Journal of Developmental Psychology, 18,* 81–96.

Spelke, E.S. (2000). Core knowledge. *American Psychologist, 55,* 1233–1243.

Spelke, E.S., & Kinzler, K.D. (2007). Core knowledge. *Developmental Science, 10,* 89–96.

Spelke, E.S., Phillips, A., & Woodward, A.I. (1995). Infants' knowledge of object and human action. In D. Sperber, D. Premack, & A. Premack (Eds.), *Causal cognition: A multidisciplinary debate* (pp. 44–78). Oxford, England: Clarendon Press.

Stipek, D. (2008). The price of inattention to mathematics in early childhood education is too great. *Society for Research in Child Development Social Policy Report, 22,* 13.

Strickland, D.S., & Riley-Ayers, S. (2006, April). Early literacy: Policy and practice in the preschool years. *NIEER Preschool Policy Brief, 10.* New Brunswick, NJ: National Institute for Early Education Research. Retrieved April 20, 2009, from http://nieer.org/resources/policybriefs/10.pdf

Sylva, K., Siraj-Blatchford, I., & Taggart, B. (2006). *Assessing quality in the early years: Early Childhood Environment Rating Scale Extension (ECERS-E).* Stoke-on-Trent, England: Trentham Books.

Templin, M.C. (1957). *Certain language skills in children.* Minneapolis: University of Minnesota Press.

Wurm, W. (2005). *Working in the Reggio way: A beginner's guide for American teachers.* St. Paul, MN: Redleaf Press.

Vygotsky, L.S. (1962). *Thought and language.* Cambridge, MA: The MIT Press.

Zur, O., & Gelman, R. (2004). Young children can add and subtract by predicting and checking. *Early Childhood Research Quarterly, 19,* 121–137.

Index

Page references followed by *b, t, f,* or *n* indicate boxes, tables, figures, or footnotes, respectively.